NEBS
MANAGEMENT
DEVELOPMENT

SUPER SERIES

THIRD EDITION
Managing Information

Making and Taking Decisions

Published for

&**NEBS** Management *by*

Pergamon
Open
Learning

Pergamon Open Learning
An imprint of Butterworth-Heinemann
Linacre House, Jordan Hill, Oxford OX2 8DP
A division of Reed Educational and Professional Publishing Ltd

ℛ A member of the Reed Elsevier plc group

OXFORD   BOSTON   JOHANNESBURG
MELBOURNE   NEW DELHI   SINGAPORE

First published 1986
Second edition 1991
Third edition 1997

British Library Cataloguing in Publication Data
A catalogue record for this book is available from the British Library

ISBN 0 7506 3333 6

The views expressed in this work are those
of the authors and do not necessarily reflect
those of the National Examining Board for
Supervision and Management or of the publisher.

NEBS Management Project Manager: Diana Thomas
Author: Howard Senter
Editor: Petra Kopp
Series Editor: Diana Thomas
Based on previous material by: Joe Johnson and William Tait
Composition by Genesis Typesetting, Rochester, Kent
Printed and bound in Great Britain

Contents

Reflect and review

Workbook introduction

1 NEBS Management Super Series 3 study links

Here are the workbook titles in each module which link with *Making and Taking Decisions*, should you wish to extend your study to other Super Series workbooks. There is a brief description of each workbook in the User Guide.

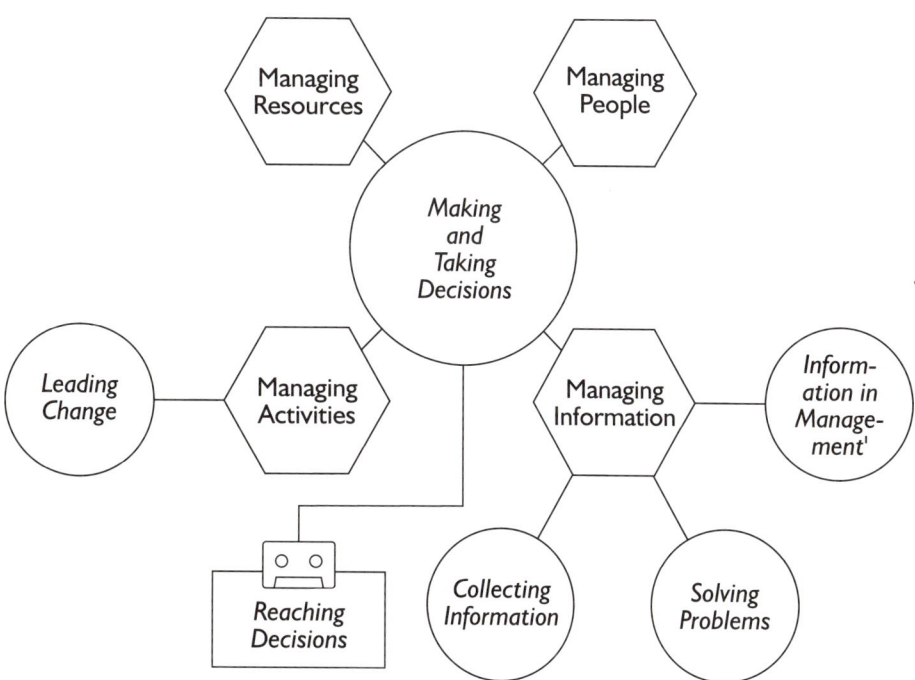

2 S/NVQ links

This workbook relates to the following elements:

C1.1   Develop your own skills to improve your performance
D1.1   Gather required information

It is designed to help you to demonstrate the following Personal Competences:

- thinking and taking decisions;
- influencing others.

3 Workbook objectives

Leadership is about making decisions, and managers, supervisors and team leaders are faced with decisions all the time.

Management decision making is closely linked to problem solving, and it plays an absolutely crucial role in two ways.

Every day there are decisions to be made about all kinds of operational matters. Mostly these are small issues, and there isn't very much time to think about them. But there are also decisions on which a great deal depends: quality of products and services, costs, revenues, productivity, market success, working relationships and people's careers. These are important decisions that can change the shape of the future, and the consequences of making the wrong decision can be severe.

It pays to take time to think such decisions through:

- What do we hope to achieve?
- What are the options?
- Which is the best option?
- How do we make it work?

In the four sessions that follow, these ideas will be developed into a formula for systematic decision making. You will work through this formula and see how it can be used in practice.

The workbook starts by explaining how the problem-solving and decision-making processes are linked. It develops a systematic step-by-step formula for making decisions. An important part of this formula is thinking about how to go about setting objectives and criteria that will help you make the best choice between the options available to you. And since good decision making depends very much on having relevant and reliable information, you'll be thinking about how to collect and evaluate such information. Finally, you'll get some guidance on implementing decisions.

3.1 Objectives

When you have completed this workbook you will be better able to:

- adopt a systematic and thoughtful approach to making difficult decisions;
- understand what makes good and bad decisions;
- set and prioritize objectives for decisions;
- identify constraints on your decisions;
- develop and evaluate decision options;
- implement decisions and evaluate outcomes.

4 Activity planner

The following activities require some planning so you may want to look at these now.

Activity 4 asks you to begin compiling a selection of decisions that you have made. The sooner you can begin this, the better; the activity will also be relevant to Activity 16 and your Work-based assignment (see page 68).

Activity 23 asks you to compile a directory of information sources that will enable you to get quicker access to the information you need for decision making.

Portfolio of evidence

Activities 4, 10, 16, 23 and 31 and the Work-based assignment may also form the basis of appropriate evidence for your S/NVQ portfolio. All Portfolio Activities and the Work-based assignment are signposted with this icon.

The icon states the elements to which the Portfolio Activities and Work-based assignment relate.

The Work-based assignment (on page 68) asks you to analyse and evaluate three important decisions you have recently made in the course of your work. You might like to start thinking about your selection now.

Session A Decisions large and small

1 Introduction

The main difference that sets supervisors and managers apart from other employees is the kind and number of decisions that they make. In fact, we might say that **management is about decision making**.

Easy or difficult, all decisions change the way the future will look. They involve making judgements, based on understanding, and the better your understanding, the better chance you have of making sound judgements.

■ At the depot, Mark was wondering what to do. Over 20 per cent of his staff were absent this morning. How could he run a normal service with so many people away?

■ On June's line in the toy factory, work had come to a stop. The quality control department had rejected the whole of the last batch of work. June knew she had to get to the bottom of the problem – there was no quick and easy answer to this one. Meanwhile, her team were sitting and chatting, awaiting her decision …

■ Fazal had been called in to see the manager. Apparently the deadline for delivering the new designs had been brought forward a week. Fazal listened, wondering how he could juggle priorities to meet the demand and still keep his promises to his team to cut down the hours they had to work.

■ In the bakery department, it wasn't only the heat from the ovens making Joyce feel hot under the collar. She felt she just couldn't work alongside Mavis any longer, after what she'd said. Joyce decided to take her problem to the supervisor …

You probably have to deal with problems like these all the time – and to find solutions you'll nearly always have to make some decisions along the way.

To start this workbook we will look at:

■ the relationship between decision making and problem solving;
■ easy and hard decisions;
■ how people make decisions; and
■ good and bad decisions.

You will also be introduced to a formula for thoughtful decision making that will guide you through the remainder of the workbook.

2 Problems and decisions

When we think of decisions, we generally think in terms of the 'tough ones' – decisions that are difficult to make.

■ Debra had a problem. She had arranged to get away early to pick up her daughter from the child-minder and take her to a friend's party. She was just getting ready to go when the office called and told her to do an urgent report on an incident the previous day. It had to be in the post by 5 pm, which would make her late picking up the child, who would then miss the party.

Activity 1

What exactly is Debra's problem?

_____

_____

_____

Debra's problem is difficult. She has two options that seem to be mutually exclusive:

■ EITHER she needs to find a way of doing the report on time **and** picking up her daughter;
■ OR she needs to decide **between** the two tasks, in which case she must somehow 'cover' for her failure to do the other.

As this example shows, the problem-solving and decision-making processes run together: solving a problem generally means taking a decision.

Solving Problems, another Super Series workbook, written in conjunction with this one, deals with problem solving in more detail. The process described in that workbook can be summarized as follows.

2.1 A problem-solving checklist

The process of problem solving begins with recognizing and identifying a problem, and it ends with implementing the decisions that flow from it.

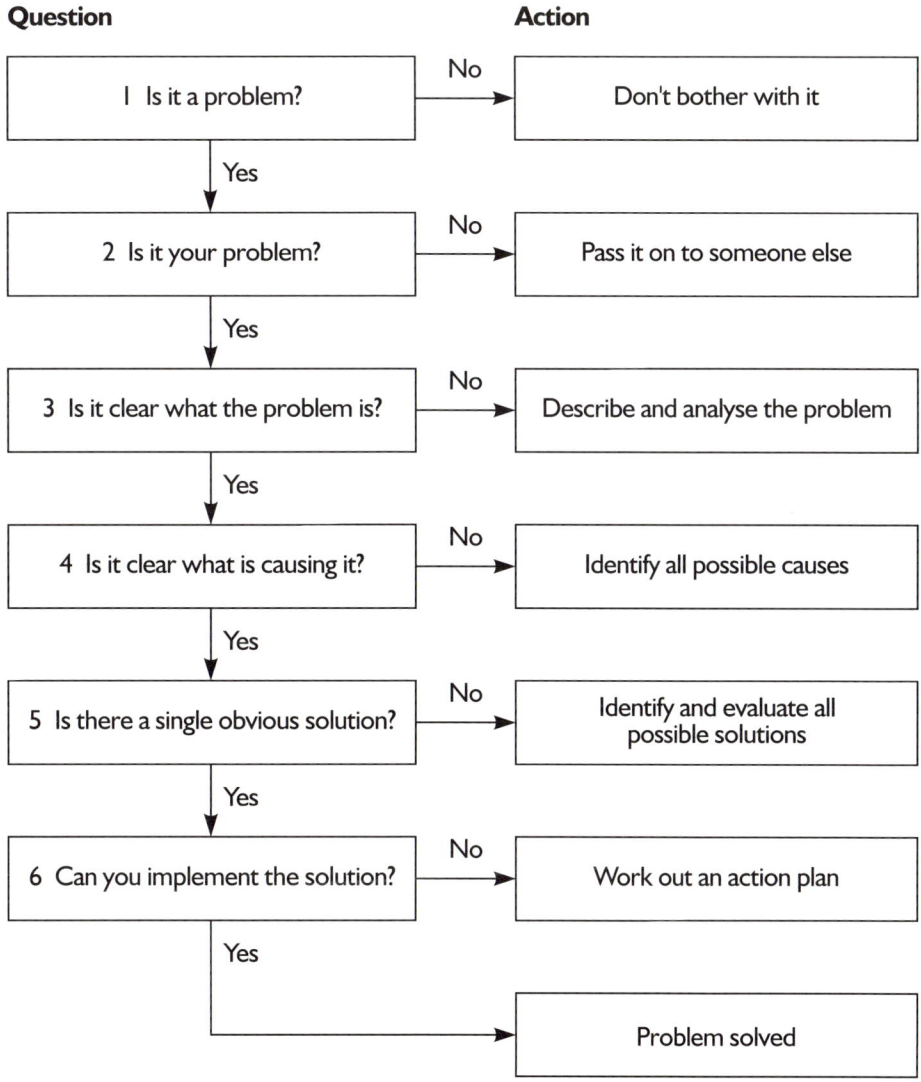

In this workbook we will be concentrating on stages 5 and 6 in this checklist, because this is where the decision making comes in.

2.2 Small and easy decisions

When you are making a **difficult decision**, based on a **problem** of some kind, it is advisable to take your time and work it through systematically. Most decisions are not of that kind, however, and they do not necessarily come about as a result of a problem.

Activity 2

3 mins

Give a couple of examples of decisions that you wouldn't describe as involving a problem.

_____

_____

_____

The tramp lay day-dreaming in the sun. 'Now, if I was rich, would I drive to the DSS in the Bentley or would I take the Rolls? Ah ... decisions, decisions!'

As you may have observed, we all have to make fairly **small and easy** decisions all the time. We decide what to wear, what to eat for lunch, whether or not to invite someone for a drink – in fact we all take countless decisions about things we seldom think of as problems.

This happens at work, too. To an experienced and well-trained manager a lot of day-to-day decisions will be very easy. They can make them **quickly** and without the need for much **conscious thought**. Exactly the same decision may present a major difficulty for a less experienced member of the team.

3   How difficult are decisions?

We have made a distinction between decisions **requiring thought** and decisions that can be made **without much thought**. You might say that this was the difference between simple decisions and complex decisions.

3.1 Complexity

Clearly, some decisions are more complex than others.

Activity 3

6 mins

How would you rate the following 'decision' situations for difficulty? Give each one a rating from 1 to 10, where 1 means very easy and 10 means very difficult.

1 You are given a choice of tea or coffee.

2 You need to decide whether to pay cash for an item or to use your credit card.

3 You have been told that one of your team must go. You now have to decide who should be made redundant.

4 You have been offered a new job in another department. You know that your team members don't want you to take it. You are torn between loyalty to your team and a desire to see the job through on the one hand, and a desire for promotion on the other.

5 Your manager has given you three important tasks to do and has set a deadline on each one. You feel there's no one to whom you could delegate any of the tasks, and at the same time you have to carry out your normal management tasks. At home there are a number of matters requiring your urgent attention. Apart from all this, you haven't been feeling well and you would dearly like to take a holiday. One thing is clear: you won't manage to achieve every-thing. You've got to make up your mind where your priorities lie.

6 A new set of work procedures has been agreed, and your manager tells you that you have three months to decide how to get your team and work area organized for the changes. This is plenty of time, providing you start planning now.

There are no right or wrong answers here. The way you rated these problems depends on your own interpretation and on what sort of decisions you are used to making. For example, perhaps most people would rate the first one – the choice between tea or coffee – as a trivial decision, and give it a rating of 1. But if you don't happen to drink tea or coffee, the decision may become impossible!

Let's consider the others.

2 This is a personal choice, probably affecting no one else. There may be a number of factors to think about – how much cash you have, whether you've exceeded your card credit limit and so on. My rating would be 2.

3 This is a terrible choice to make. No matter what you do, someone has to get bad news. I'd rate this at 9 or 10.

4   Again, there are others involved, but the decision probably isn't anywhere near as difficult as the previous problem. My rating would be 5 or 6.

5   This decision is complicated by all the factors involved. Some people might feel this to be a very stressful situation and find the decision hard to make. Others might remark that it sounded like their normal day! Rating 6 or 7 in my view.

6   This situation probably involves a number of decisions. However, time is on your side. Because of this, I would rate the difficulty at about 5 or 6.

Portfolio of evidence D1.1

Activity 4

20 mins

This Activity may provide the basis of appropriate evidence for your S/NVQ portfolio. If you are intending to take this course of action, it might be better to write your answers on separate sheets of paper.

Make a list of recent decisions that you have found difficult. (You can include decisions from private life as well as from work.)

You will need a separate sheet of paper (or use your personal organizer or computer).

Collect at least ten such decisions, and for each one note down:

■   whether or not you could see clear choices before you;
■   what the main choices were;
■   what decision you made, and why.

Why did you find these decisions so hard to make?

Different decisions can be difficult for different reasons. Generally speaking, decisions are harder to make when:

■   you lack the relevant experience;
■   you can't see clear choices;
■   other people are involved;
■   there are many aspects to consider;
■   time is short;
■   a lot is riding on the decision;
■   the situation is non-routine.

Activity 5

Consider these two problems:

1 Roy was in the middle of doing some calculations at his computer terminal, when suddenly the screen went blank. He needed to take some action to try to recover his data, but he didn't know how best to proceed.

2 Rhoda needed to get three large boxes of samples and publicity materials delivered to Madrid within twenty-four hours. She knew there were various ways of doing this, but couldn't work out which would be best.

Suggest two practical ways in which Roy and Rhoda could have reached a decision about how to proceed?

_____

_____

_____

_____

Many decisions are made easier for us because we can refer to **standard procedures** – rules, guidelines, manuals and so on. The point of these is that they lay down the best choice to make in the circumstances without individuals needing to spend time thinking about the decision.

If Rhoda's organization had 'despatch' guidelines, she could simply consult them. If Roy had a manual for his computer, he could look up the trouble-shooting guide to find out what to do.

There is another good option – **ask someone who knows the answer.** (As people develop expertise they become precious storehouses of knowledge and wisdom.)

There's a useful lesson here:

don't bother struggling with a problem or a decision if there are procedures, manuals or people that can show you what to do.

4 How people make decisions

Assuming that we don't have a set of appropriate guidelines to make the decision for us what do we do?

4.1 Decision options

In making any decision we are faced with a choice of options which we can give more or less consideration.

Activity 6

Niraj was faced with a small problem. Staff were continually snagging their clothes against a sharp corner on a filing cabinet. He had four options. Which would you favour, and why?

a move the cabinet to a different position;
b have it replaced;
c warn staff to take more care;
d ignore the matter.

This looks like a small problem, but it's quite a complicated one.

Niraj could choose any of the four options, or more than one – for example both moving the cabinet and warning staff.

Niraj may be reluctant to have the cabinet replaced because of the cost implications. However, the other options carry a risk: if the cabinet can damage clothes, it can also injure people, and sooner or later it will.

Moving the cabinet **may** solve the problem, but will not necessarily do so (it depends what exactly the problem is). If an injury occurs, Niraj could be in trouble. He may think that warning staff will get him off the hook, but this is also not necessarily so.

A stitch in time saves nine!

Ignoring the matter – which may seem an attractive option in busy times – is certain to lead to trouble in the end. And in the meantime, staff will be justifiably angry that he is ignoring their complaints.

Small problems have a habit of becoming big ones if they're not dealt with promptly.

However, there may be times and situations when experience tells you that doing nothing is not only acceptable but is actually the best option.

■ One of Tessa's staff was a habitual complainer. She complained about almost every aspect of the job. Tessa knew from past experience that her complaints rarely had substance and that, if she simply listened sympathetically, the complaints usually vanished (soon to be replaced by others, of course). If she was to react to every complaint, this would take up a lot of Tessa's valuable time, but the team member would be no happier. So Tessa didn't ignore the complaints, but for most of the time she made a conscious decision to do nothing about them.

Also, it may be wise on occasions to **postpone** a decision until further information is available.

4.2 Decision-making styles

How to actually reach a decision will vary depending on the particular problem, the context and your own management style.

Activity 7

Which of the following would you choose as the best approach to decision making?

■ Making all decisions personally, without reference to anyone else.   ☐

■ Asking the team to vote on decisions.   ☐

■ Not taking a decision until every team member has agreed to it.   ☐

■ Consulting some team members, if appropriate in the circumstances.   ☐

■ Consulting all team members from time to time, but retaining the right to the last word on the subject.   ☐

■ Taking an approach dependent on the people, the problem and the circumstances.   ☐

These options can be placed on a 'continuum' or sliding scale from 'very autocratic' to 'very democratic'. However, you may agree that the last one is generally the best approach. The extent to which a supervisor consults his or her team should depend on the people involved, the issue to be dealt with and the particular circumstances.

Having said that, decision-making styles vary from person to person. Let's look at the two extremes.

Some managers like to involve their workteams in every possible decision. This 'democratic' approach can work very well for some groups, because 'being involved' is a great motivator.

However, there is a danger in taking things too far in this direction:

- the more people are involved in a decision, the longer it generally takes to come to an agreement;
- group decisions tend to be conservative and unadventurous, but sometimes a situation calls for boldness and enterprise.

Activity 8

5 mins

Some managers are 'autocratic' and take the line 'I'm in charge, so I'll make all the decisions.' This method may seem attractive to someone who wants to appear strong and 'masterful', but it is often a poor choice.

Think about the 'autocratic' approach:

a What advantages might it have?

_____

_____

_____

b What disadvantages might it have?

_____

_____

_____

The autocratic approach is really only useful in emergencies and other situations where firm decisions are needed quickly.

It is a lot less useful in most other situations. By not involving the team, the autocrat may be ignoring a wealth of experience and knowledge. What's more, the autocratic approach may widen the divide between manager and workteam, leader and led. People usually recognize when urgent and definite leadership is appropriate, but when it isn't, they don't like it. For example, where large-scale changes in working life are at stake, an autocratic approach can cause resentment and even strengthen resistance.

4.3 Good and bad decisions

Everybody makes a great deal of decisions every day, both at work and at home, and many of those decisions will turn out to be successful. But there will always be some that prove to be less than satisfactory.

Activity 9

4 mins

What would you say adds up to a 'good' decision?

_____

_____

_____

Most people would say something like 'one that works' or 'one that solves the problem'. This is true as far as it goes, but it isn't really enough. There may be several decisions that would 'work' or solve the problem, but some might work 'better' than others. For example, they might be:

- easier to implement;
- more acceptable to the people concerned;
- more in line with the organization's policy;
- likely to create fewer unwanted side-effects;
- likely to result in a larger 'gain'.

A 'good decision' should be the **optimum** decision (i.e. the best all-round in terms of simplicity, side-effects, gain etc.) that **at least meets the minimum objectives**.

This implies that there should be objectives when decisions are being made, but we'll come back to that later.

	Objectives	Evaluation
GOOD DECISION	■ achieved sooner than expected and extra benefits gained	best outcome!
	■ achieved sooner than expected	better outcome!
	■ achieved as expected	good outcome!
LESS GOOD DECISION	■ achieved, but with unexpected undesirable side-effects	disappointing outcome
	■ only partly achieved	poor outcome
BAD DECISION	■ not achieved to any significant degree	bad outcome
	■ not achieved and more problems created	very bad outcome

Bear in mind that good decisions can be spoiled, and bad decisions made worse, by bad implementation.

	Good outcome	**Bad outcome**
Well implemented	leads to extra benefits	minimizes the damage or loss
Badly implemented	reduces the value of the achievement	exacerbates the damage or loss

4.4 Wrong decisions

Nobody is right all the time but we **can** reduce the number of times we make the wrong decision.

Portfolio of evidence C1.1, D1.1

Activity 10

4 mins

This Activity may provide the basis of appropriate evidence for your S/NVQ portfolio. If you are intending to take this course of action, it might be better to write your answers on separate sheets of paper.

Perhaps you can think of an occasion when a decision you made turned out to be an unwise one? Can you recall what went wrong? What could you have done to prevent this happening? Jot down what you can recollect about it. If you are collecting evidence for your S/NVQ portfolio, you need to identify and analyse five to ten decisions.

_____

_____

_____

_____

_____

Bad or wrong decisions can arise from a number of reasons:

■ Acting impulsively (not thinking the problem through).
■ Not having enough information to make a sound judgement. This may be due to the decision maker not making enough effort to gather together all the facts, the required information simply not being available or lack of time to collect the needed information.

■ Not having a clear idea of what the decision is meant to achieve. For instance, thinking back to Fazal's problem about revising the work rota which was mentioned on page 1 – the revised work rota – the decision depends very much on the desired outcome. One desired outcome would be **to try to keep the team happy at all costs**. Another might be **to achieve maximum efficiency, regardless of personal feelings**. Yet another might be **to keep costs down to the minimum**. Until you define your desired outcome, you can't make a good decision.

■ Not considering all the options.

5 A step-by-step formula for decision making

The step-by-step formula for 'thinking' decisions introduced in this section will be used throughout the remainder of the workbook.

Let's assume that you've already defined the problem and carried out the first four stages in the problem-solving checklist shown on page 3.

Our decision-making formula has seven stages:

I   state the **issue** or problem
O   decide **objectives**
C   identify **constraints**
I   collect **information**
O   evaluate **options**
I   **implement** the best option
O   evaluate the **outcome**.

If you have studied the workbook *Solving Problems*, you will realize that the above formula is somewhat different. This is because, while problem solving and decision making often go together, this workbook is only concerned with the decision-making end of the process. The formula therefore breaks down decision making into more stages and greatly simplifies aspects related to problem solving.

5.1   When an issue becomes a problem

The first stage refers to **issues** as well as **problems** because often you will be making decisions about things that aren't really problems as such.

Take Jerome, whose section was being moved to a new floor. He was told to lay out the working area for his team as he thought fit, provided he observed certain health and safety rules (width of walkways, fire exits etc.).

One very effective way to turn a difficult task into a problem is to put off tackling it as long as possible!

Technically, this is called an **optimization** or **improvement** problem. Jerome has the opportunity to make decisions that will get the best from the situation – the optimum layout for comfort, efficiency and so on. However, most people would see this is a 'task' or a 'job' rather than a problem. If Jerome finds the task particularly difficult, however, he may think of it as a problem.

5.2 Applying the formula

You may find it strange that the word 'decision' doesn't appear in the decision-making formula above. That's because the actual decision – the choice between options – is the easy part. Once you've done everything else, the right decision should be fairly obvious.

Here's an example.

■ Annette was in charge of the charity's administration department and had seven other people working under her. She was told that money was getting tighter and that she would be expected to find savings of 15 per cent of running costs for the coming year, with no reduction in workload. She was given two weeks to present her recommendations. Annette isn't personally making the decision, but her advice will be followed by the person who does.

Here is how she proceeded.

Stage		Conclusions
I	she stated the **issue** or problem clearly	Required to reduce the running costs of the department by 15 per cent over the next full year, i.e. get them down from approx. £97,000 to approx. £82,500
O	she decided her **objectives**	■ MUST find cost savings of £14,500; ■ MUST be able to handle same workload; ■ OUGHT TO avoid damaging morale unduly; ■ OUGHT TO avoid redundancies; ■ WOULD LIKE to use this opportunity to introduce more flexible working practices

C	she identified the **constraints**	■ no compulsory redundancies (agreement to this effect with staff association); ■ recommendation must be made within two weeks; ■ redundancy payments, if any, must not exceed £5000
I	she collected **information**	■ full details of departmental costs, including what direct costs were included in the £97,000; ■ each person's employment costs, main roles and a brief appraisal of their performance; ■ any activities duplicated elsewhere in the charity; ■ possible savings by putting some staff on part-time contracts
O	she evaluated **options**	1 Save the required sums out of admin. and overhead costs, not salaries: not possible, these only amount to 17 per cent of departmental costs, so almost all would have to go; small savings could perhaps be made. 2 Make the highest-paid team member (after herself) redundant: this would save the requisite sum, but might not be possible (no compulsory redundancies) unless the person was willing to leave; £5000 (the maximum redundancy payment) might be too little to achieve this. 3 Ask two team members to go part-time: would not save quite enough, but might work if some savings could also be made on other costs (see option 1); would depend on willingness of individuals to volunteer. 4 Ask everyone to take a 15 per cent pay cut: a more difficult task; staff in other departments might object.

This was as far as Annette was required to go for the moment; she drew up her proposals and submitted them to management. Her recommendation was to try option 3. In due course she was asked to put the decision into effect:

	Stage	Action
I	she **implemented** the chosen option	Annette found two members of the team who were willing to try a job-share, in which one would work two days and the other three. She made savings on paper and phone calls, and cancelled a training course and a replacement computer that she had budgeted for. This enabled her to reach the desired 15 per cent reduction.
O	she evaluated the **outcome**	After three months, Annette reviewed the job-sharing arrangement. It seemed to be going smoothly enough. On the other hand, her planned savings on paper and telephones hadn't materialized, and there was some resentment about her cancelling the training course and the new computer. In general, Annette thought, the decision and its implementation had been fairly satisfactory.

In the next three sessions of the workbook we'll examine all of the steps in more detail.

Self-assessment 1

1   Fill in the blanks in the following sentences with suitable words.

a   Decisions mostly involve making _____ , based on _____.
    The better your understanding, the better chance you have of making sound
    _____.

b   Decisions are harder when:
    ■ you lack the relevant _____;
    ■ you can't see clear _____;
    ■ other _____ are involved;

- there are many _____ to consider;

- _____ is short;

- a lot is riding on the _____;

- the situation is non-_____.

c No one decision-making _____ is appropriate for all circumstances.

2 Say whether the following statements are true or false. If they are false, explain why.

a As a general rule, you shouldn't waste time on decision making until a problem has reached a point where you can no longer ignore it.

_____

_____

b Apparently effortless decisions made about complex subjects are invariably based on being clever.

_____

_____

c Doing nothing is never an option.

_____

_____

d A manager who is too 'democratic' may sometimes find that required decisions take much longer than desired.

_____

_____

3 Which **two** of the following statements are the most common reasons for making wrong decisions?

a Acting without thought. ☐

b Not having enough information. ☐

c Having too many options and too little time. ☐

d Having too much time and too few options. ☐

Answers to these questions can be found on pages 76–7.

6 Summary

- **Decisions** mostly involve making **judgements**, based on **understanding**. The better your understanding, the better chance you have of making sound judgements.

- Decisions are harder when:
  - you lack the relevant **experience**;
  - you can't see clear **choices**;
  - other **people** are involved;
  - there are many **aspects** to consider;
  - **time** is short;
  - a lot is riding on the **decision**;
  - the situation is non-**routine**.

- To make good decisions, you need to define what you want and expect from the **outcome**.

- No one decision-making **style** is appropriate for all circumstances.

- The steps for making good decisions can be set out as:
  - I   state the **issue** or problem
  - O   decide **objectives**
  - C   identify **constraints**
  - I   collect **information**
  - O   evaluate **options**
  - I   **implement** the best option
  - O   evaluate the **outcome**.

Session B Issues, objectives and constraints

1 Introduction

This session covers the first three stages of the decision-making formula:

I   state the **issue** or problem
O   decide **objectives**
C   identify **constraints**

All management decisions are made for the same general reason: to ensure that the organization's goals are met. That may mean:

■   steering activities back onto track;
■   preventing a problem from developing;
■   planning improvements for the future;
■   making optimum choices for future directions.

Whichever it is, it's impossible to get down to serious decision making until you're clear what the issue actually is. This may often be obvious, but lots of issues are complex and there may be many aspects to consider.

When you have brought the issue clearly into focus, the next step is to define your objectives. Having objectives helps decision makers to focus on the issues and, following implementation, to judge whether the decision has succeeded.

You will never be free to make any decision you like, however. Decisions are always subject to constraints – limits of various kinds within which the decision must be framed.

2 Stating the issue

I   state the **issue** or problem

2.1 Recognizing that an issue exists

The notion of recognizing or 'acknowledging' that an issue or problem exists really belongs under the heading of 'solving problems' and is covered in detail in the workbook with that title. However, two points are particularly relevant to the subject of this workbook.

Managers, supervisors and team leaders need to be able to:

■   recognize when an issue or problem exists;
■   anticipate issues or problems that may arise in the future.

■   Andrea was in charge of an accounts office that processed thousands of invoices a month. Over a period of time she had become vaguely aware that the work was taking longer to do, that everyone seemed to be more harassed and short-tempered, and that when anyone was sick or taking part in training the situation got quite chaotic. Andrea herself was spending more and more time helping to complete batches of invoices, or dealing with queries and complaints about items that hadn't yet been processed.

Eventually, one of her staff took her aside and said 'Look, Andrea, we can't go on like this, you know. We're handling a quarter as much again as we were doing last year, and they're always complaining that we're getting behind. Can't you get us some more staff?'

Andrea was astonished. 'A quarter as much again! I don't believe it.' 'You just check', said her colleague, 'We're averaging nearly 12,000 a month, and it was only about 9500 this time last year.'

Activity 11

Why do you think Andrea hadn't noticed what was happening?

_____

_____

What would you say was the issue or problem requiring a decision here?

_____

_____

It may seem odd that the person in charge wouldn't realize that the number of invoices being processed had risen so much. But when your life is spent rushing around, organizing people and 'firefighting' (dealing with endless small crises), it's quite possible to lose sight of the overall picture.

Andrea – like so many people in that kind of position – would have done better to spend some time thinking about the situation, or discussing it with her team, rather than rushing around 'managing'.

Broadly, the issue is what Andrea can do to reduce her department's excessive workload, but the situation is quite complicated. By allowing it to go on for so long, Andrea has:

- given her superiors the message that she and her team can cope;
- allowed her credibility with the team to suffer.

Not for the first time in history, the 'troops' recognized a problem and the 'officer' didn't. Andrea has failed to carry out one of her key tasks as a team leader – to look after her team's interests.

Activity 12

We can state the issue as follows: **what can Andrea do to reduce her department's excessive workload?**

Try to express it in more specific terms, as if you were Andrea, trying to get clear in your head what it is you have to do.

_____

_____

_____

_____

_____

_____

_____

_____

_____

_____

All the information is in the case study, but it may help to spell it out logically:

Beware of becoming so concerned about small issues that you lose sight of the big ones, or 'make sure you can see the wood as well as the trees'.

1 Over the last year, the workload has increased by around 25 per cent.

2 The manager and the team are under too much strain.

3 As a result there are delays, increased error rates (and probably, though we don't have direct evidence here) morale problems and increased absenteeism and staff turnover.

4 The workload should therefore be decreased.

5 However, it may be difficult to convince senior management to take the necessary action.

2.2 The value of writing it down

Sometimes it's obvious what the issue is. If a machine breaks down, the issue is getting it repaired, and possibly switching work elsewhere. Not all issues are so simple, though. Andrea's case is far from simple. She has problems with the workteam, problems with the work, and she is about to have problems with her boss.

The simple fact of 'putting it in writing' often makes a problem disappear, or it can at least make a number of solutions spring to mind.

Describing complex issues in writing often helps:

■ it forces you to think;
■ it gives you a clear statement on which you can focus your attention;
■ it helps you see where the main difficulties lie.

A good start is to take a blank sheet of paper and write down the heading:

This is the issue: _____

_____

_____

It's also useful to make a note of the key facts, such as:

Expressing thoughts in writing can help turn vague ideas into concrete plans.

■ when the issue first arose (particularly if it is a 'problem');
■ who was/is involved;
■ the likely consequences if it isn't dealt with;
■ any other relevant facts.

Jot down facts and ideas in whatever order they occur to you (you can sort them into logical order later). Then turn your thoughts on yourself.

■ Did you fail to recognize a problem?

If so, do you need to take a different attitude to things in future?

■ Did you delay dealing with the issue, even after you recognized it?

If so, why, and what were the consequences? Can you make yourself deal with issues more promptly in future?

■ Is anything holding you back from dealing with the issue now?

Lack of confidence, discomfort with this particular issue, poor time management, fear of making things worse?

You may learn the skills of problem solving and decision making, but that may still leave some **personal competences** that you urgently need to review and develop.

2.3 Watching out for emerging problems

You already know that people with management responsibilities constantly need to be on the lookout for potential problems. It's far better to smother such problems at birth than to let a situation develop into a crisis.

Activity 13

How can you anticipate problems?

Think about the problems you've had to deal with recently. Try to pinpoint one that arose gradually, or developed from very small beginnings.

Jot down the signs that warned you (or should have warned you, in retrospect) that a problem was starting to emerge.

_____

_____

_____

_____

_____

Depending on the kind of work you do, there may be any number of signs of an emerging problem, including:

- team members behaving out of character;
- a process varying more than usual;
- inconsistent performance for no apparent reason;
- management reorganizations;
- a change of function or objectives;
- a cycle of events which has led to problems on previous occasions;
- a change of personnel.

In fact, a change of any kind, whether in a recognized pattern of events or in behaviour, may indicate that problems are looming. This is true both of the **working environment** and of **people's moods**, both things to which most managers, supervisors and team leaders should be sensitive.

> The fire that gutted Norwich City Library in 1995, destroying priceless wartime archives, was caused by a faulty plug overheating. Did no one notice that tell-tale smell of overheating plastic in the days before the fire broke out?

- Everyone was used to the quiet humming and clicking of the network file server in the main office. One afternoon, Mervyn gradually noticed a change in its tone. There was a small, but distinct, background vibration that varied slightly every few minutes. Mervyn phoned the IT help-desk, who sent a computer engineer to check. 'Good job you called me', he said. 'The cooler fan on the main processor was on the blink. If you'd left it a bit longer it would have failed. Then you'd have had a right mess inside there – £2000 damage minimum, I should say.'

Good managers are always:

- monitoring;
- observing;
- comparing;
- listening;
- thinking ahead;
- ready to spot and act on small changes in the human and physical environment.

2.4 Talking issues over

Writing down is a great help, but so is talking issues over. Team members, colleagues and your manager will have most relevant comments to make. The person you talk with doesn't necessarily need to be fully versed in the technicalities – the only essential requirement is that he or she is willing to listen.

Talking it over is mainly to help you express the issue more clearly; if the other person may help you get a different 'angle' on it, that is a bonus!

Make a habit of expressing problems and other issues in words, both in writing and in speech. In due course this will help you reach better decisions.

3 Deciding your objectives

Now we're at the second step in our decision-making formula.

O decide **objectives**

If a decision is to be effective, the decision maker must be clear about what outcome is desired. This means setting objectives, which in turn means thinking hard about the issue.

Having clear and sensible objectives has two most important consequences:

- you know what you are trying to achieve, so you can focus on this and there's less chance of being side-tracked;
- when you've made and implemented your decision, you can measure how well you've done.

We can show the process like this:

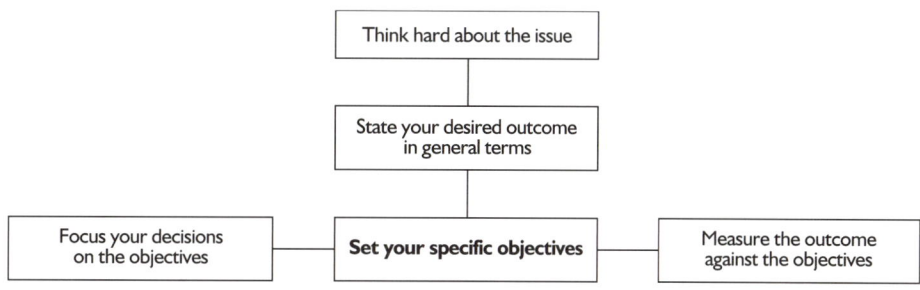

3.1 Outcomes and objectives

There is an important distinction between outcomes and objectives.

Outcomes are what actually happens as a result of the decisions you make. You usually express your **desired outcomes** briefly, in fairly broad terms. However, you may not get the outcomes that you desire!

Objectives are the specific things that you want to achieve, in order to get the outcome that you desire.

You should select objectives that, properly achieved, will deliver your desired outcomes.

Activity 14

4 mins

You have to discipline a member of your team for repeatedly being late for work. You call the member in for a disciplinary interview.

What is your desired outcome likely to be in a case like this?

_____

_____

_____

What are your specific objectives likely to be in holding the interview?

_____

_____

_____

An appropriate 'desired outcome' might be that the team member is never late again.

Your objectives may be to discover the reasons for the persistent lateness and to warn the offender of the action that might be taken if the state of affairs continues.

Yet, if they are honest, many managers might go into a disciplinary interview thinking one of the following:

■ 'This person must be punished for such behaviour.'

■ 'I must discipline this offender as an example to the others.'

■ 'If I stick to the disciplinary rules, my boss is bound to approve of my actions.'

The decisions you make depend on the objectives you select, which depend on the outcome you are aiming to achieve.

3.2 'Must', 'want' and 'would like'

If you look back to the example of Annette's decision making on pages 14–15, you'll notice that she didn't simply list two or three objectives of equal importance. She had two objectives that she labelled 'MUST' and a couple more labelled 'OUGHT TO'.

This is realistic. When you're setting objectives, there are generally two or three things that you MUST achieve in order to count the operation a success.

But there are also usually a number of other things that it would be nice, or desirable, to achieve at the same time.

There are in fact:

■ **MUST** objectives

If we don't achieve these, the decision was a bad one;

■ **WANT** objectives

Things that it is important, but not essential, to achieve (these are the 'ought to' items in Annette's list);

■ **WOULD LIKE** objectives

Things it would be nice to achieve, but which aren't really of any great importance.

These levels are important when there are several possible courses of action from which to choose.

Activity 15

5 mins

Here are some objectives relating to the 'disciplinary interview' example we used a little earlier. There are three possible courses of action from which you can choose. The objectives that each will achieve are shown by ticks. Which one is the best – A, B or C?

	Objective	A	B	C
1	MUST discover reasons for persistent lateness	✓	✓	
2	MUST warn offender of what action will be taken	✓	✓	✓
3	WANT to demonstrate to boss that I can apply the disciplinary rules correctly		✓	
4	WANT to make an example to others	✓	✓	✓
5	WOULD LIKE to punish the person	✓		✓

The best decision is: _____

A good decision, as we defined it in Session A, is: the **optimum** decision (i.e. the best all-round in terms of simplicity, side-effects, gain etc.) that **at least meets the minimum objectives**.

The MUSTs are the minimum objectives. They are **'GO/NO-GO criteria'**: any decision that does not deliver them is NO-GO. That rules out option C, because it does not discover the reason for the persistent lateness.

27

The choice is therefore between options A and B, which both deliver the minimum objectives. The best choice is probably B, because it also delivers both the WANT objectives which are the next most important. Option A delivers one WANT, plus one WOULD LIKE, which puts it below option B in rank order.

3.3 Weighted objectives

Sometimes a decision depends on quite a lot of objectives or 'decision criteria'. There may, for example, be several WANTs and WOULD LIKEs and, when you get down to thinking about them, you may feel that they are all at slightly different levels of importance.

If this is so, you can give each non-essential objective a numerical weighting to help you reach your decision. 'Weighting' simply means giving a bigger number to things that you value highly and a smaller number to less important matters. Here's an example.

■ Jack and Michel were trying to decide what new lap-top computers to supply to the paper's journalists. There were over twenty models to choose from, all with slightly different specifications. They eventually drew up a 'score-sheet' as follows:

MUST HAVE (GO/NO-GO criteria)

1   at least 8 mbytes RAM
2   at least 420 mbyte hard disk
3   Pentium 100 microprocessor chip or better
4   at least 2.5 hours battery time
5   built-in fax/modem
6   at least 9.5 inch screen

WANTs/WOULD LIKEs	weight
7 pre-installed operating system	8
8 weight under 1.8 kg	4
9 built-in mouse/trackball	9
10 microprocessor upgradeability	6
11 carrying case	5
12 maths co-processor	2
13 one-year warranty	7
14 three-year warranty	10
15 extra 4 m/bytes RAM	3
MAXIMUM TOTAL	54

Each model could be ticked off against this list. They must all match all of the MUST criteria; any that don't are ruled out. The decision therefore rests on the 'WANT/WOULD LIKE' criteria. Since not all models will offer the same range of facilities and 'extras', the total value of the 'weights' will differ. The model with the highest weighted total is the winner (providing that the price is right!).

Portfolio of evidence C1.1, D1.1

Activity 16

20 mins

This Activity may provide the basis of appropriate evidence for your S/NVQ portfolio. If you are intending to take this course of action, it might be better to write your answers on separate sheets of paper.

Practise applying this 'weighted objectives' method to some of the more complex decisions that you have recently had to make. Look back on your answer to Activity 4 on page 6 and select four of the decisions you identified there. The criteria are that there should be several WANT and WOULD LIKE objectives in the situation and two or more realistic options between which to choose.

Weigh up the decisions using this technique. Do you still come to the same decision as before?

Does listing and weighting the WANTs and WOULD LIKEs help you analyse the situation and reach your decision more efficiently?

> **EXTENSION 1**
> You may be interested in finding out more about problem solving and decision making using weighting and other numerical techniques. If so, you might consider taking up this extension, a simple but fascinating book called *The New Rational Manager*.

4 Constraints

'Constraints' are the limitations and controls which restrict our options when considering solutions to problems and reaching a decision.

Activity 17

3 mins

One common constraint is lack of time. Can you think of **two** other typical constraints which might be placed on you when making a decision at work, restricting your choice of options?

_____

_____

_____

You might have mentioned some of the following constraints.

■ **The requirements or demands of your manager**

When outlining a task, he or she may insist that you comply with certain conditions.

■ **The requirements or demands of the workteam**

For example, when given an instruction to find ways of cutting running costs, you may decide to rule out recommending a reduction in staff numbers.

■ **Not being able to find all the information you need**

■ **Lack of other resources**

■ **The limits of your authority**

Few people have unlimited authority, even within their own work area.

■ **Cost constraints**

These are perhaps the most common.

■ **Constraints due to limitations of your own ability**

We all have our limitations!

■ **Physical restraints**

Such as having to operate within a limited work area.

In addition, you may be constrained by your own conscience or beliefs, and by the 'culture' or policy of your organization.

■ One of the major problems that Marcus faced in running his large branch bookshop was staffing. Assistants had to be well-educated and bright, but the pay wasn't very good. The better assistants often left within nine months, and replacements had to be recruited. At the same time, Marcus was under pressure to reduce staffing costs (he had some flexibility in setting pay rates for new recruits). The issue was how to maintain an adequate level of customer service **and** reduce payroll costs in the face of this high staff turnover.

There were severe constraints on his decision:

■ a modest recruitment budget;
■ fixed maximums for individual salaries;
■ fixed targets for total payroll costs.

When Marcus thought about the issue, he realized that all the assistants were graduates. It occurred to him that a solution might be to advertise for A-level school leavers with good literary skills. They would be cheaper, would be likely to stay longer and, with appropriate training, would still provide the required level of service to customers.

Marcus's proposal was rejected out of hand by the personnel director. 'Our policy is to employ graduates only. That is what our customers expect – and what the existing staff expect. You'll have to find another solution.'

Thus there was an unexpected policy/cultural constraint that further limited Marcus's freedom to find a solution to the problem.

As this case study also shows, the demands and constraints placed on managers and supervisors are often **conflicting**. It is difficult, perhaps impossible, to find a solution that satisfactorily takes account of all of them.

Activity 18

4 mins

a What were the conflicting demands placed on Marcus in the situation we have just described?

_____

_____

b Think about some of the decisions you have had to make yourself. Jot down some areas where the constraints and demands placed on you seemed to be conflicting.

_____

_____

_____

_____

_____

Marcus is in a difficult position. He is required to keep down staff costs, but at the same time he has to employ highly qualified staff. He can't retain them for long because they can earn more elsewhere. Marcus's solution to the problem is vetoed by higher management. The only answer looks like the unsatisfactory one of accepting high staff turnover.

Most managers who, like Marcus, run small 'profit centres' are in the same boat. You probably noted similar conflicts between costs, quality and standards yourself.

Here's another typical situation.

■ The supervisor has been told to push up production by 5 per cent. The workteam is on a production bonus, which means they receive extra pay for producing more than a standard number of items. However, rejected items don't count, so they have to keep the quality up, too.

At the same time, the safety officer has issued instructions about safety procedures, which limit the speed at which the team can work. Other factors, such as the supply of parts, are outside the supervisor's control.

The process depends on good relations with other teams, so the supervisor spends much of her time in liaison work, whereas her team would prefer that she spent more time on dealing with their problems. She is also under time pressure because her manager demands to be kept informed of progress and all significant events.

Activity 19

List all the instances of conflicting demands and constraints that you can identify in the case study:

_____

_____

_____

_____

_____

_____

The answer to this activity can be found on page 79.

Although your work situation may be different, it is likely that your work and your decisions will be subject to just as many constraints, and that these may often be conflicting.

However, that's what being in a management role is all about: using your skills and judgement to cope with the many conflicting demands. As a consequence, most decisions involve making compromises. Few decisions leave all parties feeling completely satisfied with the outcome.

Self-assessment 2

1 Fill in the blanks in the following sentences with suitable words.

a Beware of becoming so concerned about _____ problems that you lose sight of the _____ ones.

b MUSTs are your _____ objectives, which we can also think of as GO/NO-GO _____.

c Giving non-_____ objectives a numerical_____ will often help you to reach your decision.

d Making decisions usually means making _____. Few decisions leave all parties feeling completely satisfied with the _____.

2 Comment briefly on the following statements:

a You can anticipate problems by being observant.

_____

_____

b Writing a problem down is not as helpful as talking it over with someone.

_____

_____

c You may often be constrained by lack of resources, but should not be constrained by the demands of the workteam.

_____

_____

d When your manager says 'You have a completely free hand', it means there will be absolutely no constraints on the decision you make.

_____

_____

33

3   Place these stages of the decision-making formula in the right order.

collect **information**   a _____

decide **objectives**   b _____

evaluate **options**   c _____

evaluate the **outcome**   d _____

identify **constraints**   e _____

implement the best option   f _____

state the **issue** or problem g _____

4   Setting specific objectives for a decision has two main benefits. What are they?

a _____

b _____

Answers to these questions can be found on pages 77–8.

5 Summary

■ Managers, supervisors and team leaders need to be able to:

  ■ recognize when a problem exists;
  ■ anticipate problems that may arise in the future.

■ Describing complex issues in writing:

  ■ forces you to think;
  ■ gives you a clear statement on which you can focus your attention;
  ■ helps you see where the main difficulties lie.

■ People with management responsibilities need to be on the lookout for potential problems, so that they can prevent them developing into something more serious.

■ You should make a habit of expressing problems and other issues in words, both in writing and in speech. This will help you reach better decisions.

■ Having clear and sensible objectives has two most important consequences:

  ■ you know what you are trying to achieve, so you can focus on this and there's less chance of being side-tracked;
  ■ when you've made and implemented your decision, you can measure how well you've done.

■ Objectives can be sorted into three groups:

  ■ **MUST** objectives: if these aren't achieved, the decision was a bad one;
  ■ **WANT** objectives: things that it is important, but not essential, to achieve (these are the 'ought to' items in Annette's list);
  ■ **WOULD LIKE** objectives: things it would be nice to achieve, but which aren't really of any great importance.

■ 'Constraints' are the limitations and controls that restrict your options when considering solutions to problems and reaching a decision. Common constraints include lack of time, shortage of money and other resources, and the organization's policy and culture.

Session C Finding the right option

1 Introduction

During the course of this workbook so far you have:

I stated the **issue** or problem;
O decided the **objectives**;
C identified the **constraints**.

However, there is more thinking to be done before you reach the point of making the decision. You need to:

I collect **information**;
O evaluate **options**.

These two stages, which will lead you to the point of making the decision, are the subject of this session. You will think about:

- collecting information and ideas from wherever and whomever they are available;
- listing the alternatives;
- looking ahead to see what the effects of each alternative option might be.

2 Gathering information and ideas

Information gathering can be a time-consuming business, but not always, as this case study shows.

- Andrea's team was more and more overworked (see page 20 in Session B). She herself didn't clearly recognize that there was a problem, because she was so busy 'firefighting'. A member of her team pinpointed the problem for her, and she understood it immediately. The only thing she needed to do was dig out a couple of statistics:

  - the average number of invoices processed every month (to demonstrate how the workload had increased);
  - the total number of staff employed (to demonstrate that the same number of people were processing 25 per cent more invoices).

37

Unfortunately it is not always that simple. Where the issue is complex (for example a dispute with a supplier, conflict between team members, or a disciplinary/performance problem) it may take a lot more time and effort to get at 'the facts'. Even where it is a matter of collecting fairly straightforward facts and figures, time and concentration may be called for.

Activity 20

In the case study on page 28 of Session B, Jack and Michel were trying to decide what new lap-top computers to supply to the paper's journalists. There were over twenty models to choose from, all with slightly different specifications. They decided to draw up a 'scoresheet' to make it easier to compare the various models.

What would they have to do to get the appropriate information?

_____

_____

_____

The basic source of the information is the dealers and manufacturers of the machines, but Jack and Michel would probably check one or more computer magazines first. These contain hundreds of adverts which typically list the specifications.

However, the adverts are seldom up to date, and they may not contain all the necessary information. The next step would therefore be to ask the likely suppliers for more details in the shape of printed brochures, technical data sheets and letters. Even these will probably not give all the answers, so Jack and Michel will almost certainly have to phone some of the suppliers for extra information and clarification.

In the computer market, both specifications and prices change rapidly. It would probably be necessary to re-check the details immediately before making the decision.

At times you may feel that you have more information than you can cope with. We'll explore this briefly by looking first at the **kinds** of information you may have to deal with, and then with the **sources** from which it comes.

2.1 Kinds of information

You can consider yourself lucky if you only have to deal with a modest flow of information from a limited range of sources. This is not the experience of most of today's managers.

Activity 21

4 mins

Which of the following sources of information are you expected to handle during your working day?

- Facts and opinions by word of mouth from your manager, your team and your colleagues (which may not necessarily agree). ☐

- Written reports containing information which you are expected to absorb. ☐

- Statistics in the form of charts and diagrams. ☐

- Messages or written memos. ☐

- Warnings and cautions on posters. ☐

- Videos that are part of your training and that you have to watch. ☐

- Product/service information (brochures etc.). ☐

- Technical data and specifications. ☐

Are there information sources other than those listed above? If so, write down the **two** or **three** main ones.

_____

_____

_____

'Where is the wisdom we have lost in knowledge?
Where is the knowledge we have lost in information?'

From T.S. Eliot's poem 'The Rock' (1934)

Most managers and supervisors find that they are almost swamped by information. This can present a problem in itself. Although having more information **ought** to be helpful, a lot of it will be fairly irrelevant to your needs. Sorting the 'wheat from the chaff' can be a major task in terms of both time and mental energy.

Yet when you have to make difficult decisions about complex issues, you will often find that genuinely useful information is in short supply. In fact, **most decisions at work have to be made with imperfect information.**

2.2 Sources of information

Nevertheless, decision makers have to do their best to get all the relevant information they can, in the time available.

Activity 22

4 mins

What **sources** of information are available to you? ('Sources' refers to where the information comes from, rather than what it actually is.) List at least **three**.

_____

_____

_____

_____

You may have listed some of the information sources mentioned in the previous activity. The main sources of information available to most people in your position are shown in this diagram.

EXTENSION 2
This extension expands on what sort of information you might be able to obtain from the sources.

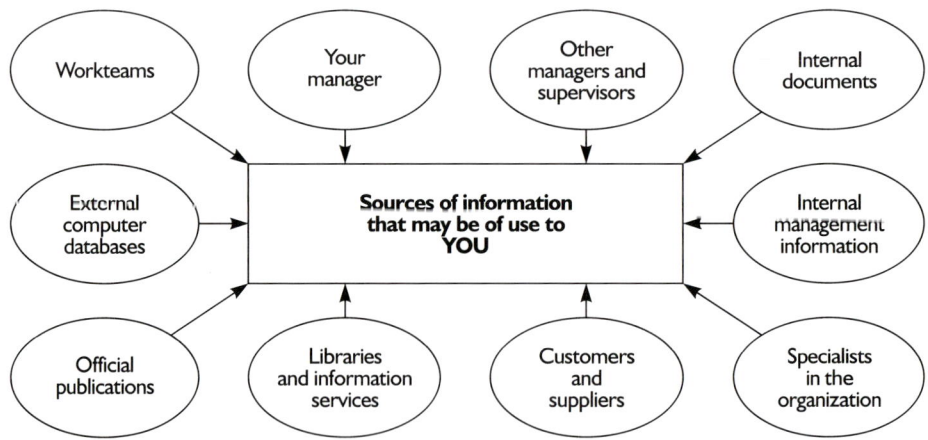

Activity 23

30 mins

This Activity may provide the basis of appropriate evidence for your S/NVQ portfolio. If you are intending to take this course of action, it might be better to write your answers on separate sheets of paper; if you have one, you could use your personal organizer, or create a database on your computer.

Start compiling a **Directory of Information Sources** to give you quicker access to information that will help you reach decisions about work-based issues.

You may need to do a little research in order to complete your directory, and it will certainly involve talking to colleagues, specialists in the organization, your manager, and possibly also outside sources such as customers and suppliers.

Step 1: List all the issues that you might need information and advice about. Here are a few to get you started, but you will have to make your own decisions, depending on your particular job and role:

- terms and conditions of employment;
- pay scales, pay policy, promotion policy;
- disciplinary rules and procedures;
- safety documentation, rules and procedures;
- personnel details of your team;
- training opportunities available;
- recruitment procedures;
- working methods and procedures;
- technical matters to do with the product or service that you provide (e.g. specifications, faults, complications, safety issues);
- technical matters to do with the equipment that you use;
- contractual terms relevant to suppliers;
- contractual terms/service agreements relevant to customers;
- output/work-rate/productivity data;
- proposals and plans for change involving you and your department;
- financial targets and budgets;
- activity/output targets and budgets.

Step 2: Make four columns (or database fields) and fill in the details as shown in the example below:

Issue	Source where?	Who?	Phone no.
Hotels suitable for use by visitors to our organization	Cramley Tourist Office	Brenda O'Neill	Cramley 213883
	'Good Hotel Guide'	MD's Secretary (Tara)	ext. 3301

2.3 Generating information of your own

Often you will need to base your decisions at least partly on calculations, which will take account of such things as:

- hourly, weekly, monthly and annual pay;
- overtime, bonus payments and productivity payments;
- staff numbers;
- working hours;
- production/activity rates;
- costs and charges of various kinds.

Look back to the issues facing Andrea in the case study on page 20. When she takes her case (which will be either for more staff or for improved equipment) to her manager, she will be asked to provide estimates of what the cost will be.

She will need to make fairly complex numerical calculations involving precisely the factors listed above.

That can be quite a challenge, but it is a common requirement for managers. Decisions involving money and output cannot be made without this sort of 'hard evidence'.

> **EXTENSION 3**
> If you want to develop your skill with spreadsheets further, *Mastering Spreadsheets, Budgets and Forecasting* by Malcolm Secrett provides a guide.

If you are going to work out your own information you need at least a calculator. But for the kind of decisions we have been talking about, where productivity, output, working hours, unit costs and pay all interlock, the only serious answer is to use a computer spreadsheet.

Making decisions often involves numbers – for example you may need to work out what the return and cost will be from various decision options. The best way to work this out, via a series of 'what if?' questions, is using a spreadsheet. Spreadsheets are covered in another workbook in the series, *Information in Management*.

2.4 Quality information

In management decision making there isn't always time for detailed scrutiny of the quality of the information you are using. You simply have to take most of it on trust. However,

the bigger the decision, the more careful you need to be about the information on which it is based.

How often can you say, in the words of W.S. Gilbert:

'Of that there is no manner of doubt, No probable, possible shadow of doubt, No possible doubt whatever.'

(From *The Gondoliers*, 1889)

It is certainly worth making a quick evaluation of the quality of your information. In broad terms, it should be:

- relevant;
- reliable;
- accurate;
- sufficiently comprehensive (in quantity and detail).

Even computer data can sometimes contain errors or be interpreted in a misleading way. How much less reliable are witness statements, reports and 'personal impressions'!

Here is a checklist to help you judge the quality of the information you have:

- Is the information relevant?

- Is it reliable?

    - Who produced it?
    - Do they have a good track record for reliability?
    - Might they be biased in any way?
    - Does the information show any signs of being biased?
    - Is it based on a fair selection of events/data?
    - Is there any other evidence to back it up?

- Is it accurate?

    - What sources were used?
    - Are there any obvious errors?
    - Are any bits missing or corrupted?

- Is it sufficiently comprehensive

    - Does it cover all the key areas?
    - Is there enough detail to make sense of the issues?

Information plays an important part in helping you to come up with decision options, and you may like to study two related workbooks in the series, *Collecting Information* and *Information in Management*.

There are also a number of creative techniques designed to aid the generation of ideas for action. This aspect of decision making, closely related to the process for solving problems, is covered in the workbook with that name.

3 Evaluating the options

Provided your search for information and ideas has been successful, you should be left with one or more options, or courses of action, that could provide a satisfactory way forward.

The task now is to compare the options, and there are three parts to this:

1   listing the alternatives;

2   thinking ahead and considering the likely effects and implications of each option;

3   making a choice.

After investigating a particular problem, most people tend to home in quickly on just one or perhaps two possible solutions. This can be a mistake, because the quality of decision making depends on having a reasonable number of options to choose from. You shouldn't dismiss any option prematurely, and new ideas may also have emerged in the light of information you've gathered.

So, before you go on to evaluate your options, it's worth 'revisiting' the issue itself:

■   Have any new possible solutions occurred to you?

■   Have you listed all the ones that originally came up?

■   Have colleagues, team members or your manager got any suggestions to add?

The next case study shows the advantage of not eliminating options too soon.

■   Mina runs a small operation 'customizing' toilet soap for the luxury gift market by personalizing and repackaging it. The work is done in a small industrial unit shared with another company. The work is labour-intensive but basically unskilled: each bar is individually pressed with the recipient's initials, wrapped by hand, tied with a ribbon and bedded on a velvet cushion in an attractive box. A gift card has to be included and then outer packaging added. A special address label has to be printed and attached.

Activity 24

■ There are two issues facing Mina: space is limited and, when the unit is working at full capacity, various regulations are being broken. However, this seldom happens because the firm can't get enough staff to do the work.

The reasons for the staff shortages are:

- the unit is on the edge of town and public transport is poor;

- wages are not very attractive – the firm says it cannot afford to pay more.

At the first attempt Mina and her manager came up with three possible solutions to these problems:

- Renting or buying a new building to provide more room to do the packing. This new building should preferably be situated nearer the centre of the town, or near the housing estates, so that it is easier for people to get to.

- Providing a bus service to collect employees from their homes.

- Paying higher wages to entice more people to do the work. (The firm says it cannot afford to pay higher wages, but can they afford not to?)

Think about the situation and see if you can come up with two or three more options.

_____

_____

_____

_____

_____

_____

_____

_____

My suggestions for this activity can be found on page 80.

3.1 Assessing feasibility

Having listed all the alternatives, how can you choose between them?

For a major project involving decisions between expensive options, it may be worthwhile to carry out **a feasibility study**.

A feasibility study is a brief investigation to find out:

- whether a proposal is realizable;
- whether it is likely to meet all the requirements;
- what 'knock-on effects' it might have.

Often, there are three main aspects to consider,

- **Technical** feasibility: the practical aspects of (say) whether a particular machine is suited to a particular job.
- **Social** feasibility: the impact on the working, personal and home lives of the people involved.
- **Economic** feasibility: estimating to what extent financial costs are balanced by financial gains.
- A fourth aspect which may come into play is the **environmental impact of a decision – its effects on the world around us**.

Activity 25

5 mins

- Roland's company has commissioned a study to look into the feasibility of introducing computer technology.

  The technical feasibility part of the study will examine such questions as what equipment is needed and to what extent computers would help to speed up the company's operations.

  The economic feasibility part of the study would try to determine how much money the company would save, considering both set-up costs and running costs.

  _____

  What would the company want to know about the social aspects of computer technology? Try to suggest **two** questions.

  _____

  _____

  _____

  _____

My response to this activity can be found on page 80.

A feasibility study may not be viable where a smaller-scale project is concerned. Nevertheless, the same kind of questions have to be answered.

- What effect will the decision have on people?
- What is the impact of the technology?
- What effect will the decision have on costs and profits?
- What impact will the decision have on the world around us?

4 Making the decision

If you have taken time and trouble over the first five steps of the decision-making formula,

I stating the **issue** or problem,
O setting your **objectives**,
C identifying **constraints**,
I collecting **information**,
O evaluating **options,**

actually taking the decision will often turn out to be comparatively painless.

If it is still difficult to come to a decision, it may be because you are in the happy position of having more than one attractive option – or alternatively that there are no attractive options.

Activity 26

3 mins

If you've followed through our step-by-step decision-making formula and still find it difficult to make a choice, it may be time to ask some searching questions, such as:

'Have I listed all the possible options?'

Try to suggest **two** further questions you might ask yourself at this stage.

_____

_____

_____

Some suggestions for further questions can be found on page 80.

One approach, if you are still unable to decide between alternative solutions to a problem, is deliberately to set up an argument. Get a friend or colleague to champion one option while you argue for another. The idea is for each person to try to persuade the other of the value of the option he or she 'owns'. **This may bring out weaknesses and strengths not appreciated before.**

Self-assessment 3

15 mins

1   The following five statements have been split in two and jumbled up. Which goes with which?

a   Before you go on to evaluate your options it's worth checking whether

b   Decisions involving money and output cannot be

c   Managers often feel that they have

d   Most decisions have to be

e   The workteam is often one of the best

v   made without making lots of numerical calculations.

w   made with imperfect information.

x   much more information than they can cope with.

y   sources of information for the supervisor.

z   colleagues, team members or your line manager have got any suggestions to add.

2   This diagram shows sources of information that are available to many people in management roles. Fill in the **five** that are missing.

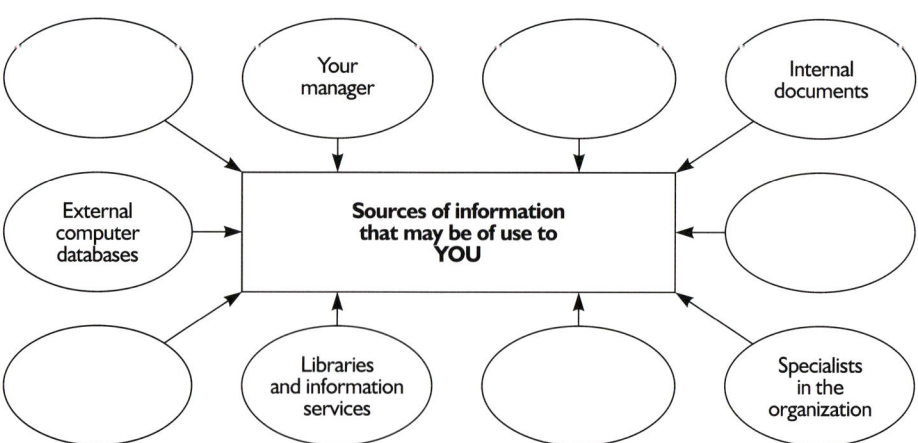

3   Feasibility studies often have four aspects. What are they?

_____

_____

_____

_____

4 Replace the missing words to give this passage its proper meaning.

In order to assess the _____ of information, you need to ask:

- Is the information _____?

- Is it _____?

- Is it _____?

- Is it sufficiently _____?

5 What should you do if you have systematically gone through all the steps of the decision-making formula and you still can't decide which solution to a problem would be the best option?

_____

_____

Answers to these questions can be found on pages 78–9.

5 Summary

- Most decisions at work have to be made with **imperfect information**. The best decision makers are the best informed ones.

- Good sources of information include the workteam, your line manager and colleagues. A wide range of other information sources also exists.

- Often so much information is available that sorting and evaluating it is a major task. At the same time the amount of **relevant** and **useful** information is often quite limited.

- Often you will need to create information of your own, particularly where the decision involves costs, revenue, working hours, output and other numerical values.

- Your information should be of reasonably good quality, i.e. relevant, reliable, accurate and sufficiently comprehensive (in quantity and detail).

- Selecting an option involves:
  - listing the alternatives;
  - thinking ahead and considering what the effects of each alternative option might be; and finally
  - making a choice.

- It is a bad idea to eliminate any possible options too soon.

- One way of choosing between alternatives is to do a feasibility study – a brief investigation to find out:

  - whether a proposal is realizable;
  - whether it is likely to meet all the requirements;
  - what 'knock-on effects' it might have.

- Decisions of all kinds may entail asking the following questions:

  - What effect will the decision have on people?
  - What is the impact of the technology?
  - What effect will the decision have on costs and profits?
  - What impact will the decision have on the world around us?

- The best option should be selected in the light of these considerations.

Session D Making it work

1 Introduction

Once your decision is finally made, it has to be put into effect. Will it survive contact with reality? Have you been making incorrect assumptions? Have you allowed for all contingencies?

After giving the decision all the thought and attention you have time for, sooner or later you have to stop thinking and start acting.

In Sessions A, B and C we dealt with the first five stages in the decision-making formula:

I   state the **issue** or problem
O   decide **objectives**
C   identify **constraints**
I   collect **information**
O   evaluate **options**

In this final session we'll consider the last two:

I   **implementing** a decision
O   assessing the **outcome**.

This will involve:

- thinking about the problems that implementation may bring;
- confirming your decision and communicating it to the people who need to know about it;
- drawing up an action plan;
- reviewing what actually happened to see what you can learn; and
- thinking ahead to the next problem and decision.

2 Preparing to implement the decision

You have now arrived at the point where the decision has to be put into effect. You still have four issues to think about:

- your ability to 'get things done';
- identifying and overcoming 'risks';
- drawing up an action plan;
- confirming the decision and informing people about it.

51

For simple decisions you won't need to bother with all of these (though informing people will always be important). When the decision is more complex, it pays to be more thorough.

2.1 The ability to get things done

Making a decision is one thing, making it happen is another. Not everyone is equally good at 'getting things done', and some people are more efficient than others. Why is this so? No one knows for sure, but it seems to be a combination of three factors:

- the individual's personality, experience and skills;
- the culture within which they operate;
- the demands of the particular situation they face.

Personal qualities certainly come into it.

Activity 27

6 mins

Which of the following would you say are typical qualities of a person who 'gets things done' at work? Tick one option from each horizontal pair.

a The ability to **establish clear goals** and to keep them firmly in mind ☐

b The **doggedness** to forge on without clear objectives. ☐

c The **independence and self-confidence** to ignore offers of help from others. ☐

d The **willingness to accept help** from others where this will help achieve the objectives. ☐

e The **courage** to take risks. ☐

f The **caution** to avoid taking risks. ☐

g The **perseverance** to pursue an objective until it is achieved. ☐

h The **realism** to recognize when goals are too difficult to be worth pursuing. ☐

i Total **belief in oneself** and a refusal to acknowledge that mistakes are possible. ☐

j The **humility** to admit mistakes and to try to learn from them. ☐

k The **willingness to learn** from the experiences of others. ☐

l The **determination** to seek one's own solutions, even if this means 're-inventing the wheel'. ☐

m The **strength** to force a decision through against all obstacles. ☐

n The **flexibility** to modify plans and overcome resistance by negotiation. ☐

52

You may have found that this activity required some thought. I would suggest that a, d, e, j, k and n are the qualities of a successful 'doer'. Some of the others may seem active and forceful, but they won't necessarily lead to success when this depends on being able to motivate a team and colleagues and convince others of your case. The choice between g and h is not clear-cut. There could be situations where either approach would be best.

Let's review those 'success' points again.

■ The ability to establish clear goals and to keep them firmly in mind.

This is vital. You often see people who are working hard, but are wasting their time because they have no clear goals, or have lost sight of them.

■ The willingness to accept help from others where this will help achieve the objectives.

Being too independent is usually a fault. Achievement at work is a team effort, and working alone makes the job much tougher. Decisions made by one person in isolation are seldom very useful, because they don't take enough account of constraints and risks. Working in this way is a sign of weakness and insecurity, not strength and leadership qualities.

■ The courage to take risks.

Timid people are not renowned for their achievements. Boldness is needed to get things done.

■ The humility to admit mistakes and to try to learn from them.

Belief in oneself is very desirable, but not if it extends to a refusal to admit one's mistakes.

■ The willingness to learn from the experiences of others.

There is no point in experimenting if the correct method or approach has already been discovered.

■ The flexibility to modify plans and overcome resistance by negotiation.

It's reasonable to persevere in reaching your objectives, but there are occasions when being a little flexible will be more effective than going like 'a bull at a gate'.

Of course, this choice of qualities is not completely cut-and-dried, nor are the qualities themselves of the 'either you've got it or you haven't' type. But effective decision making certainly is about **striking the right balance**.

■ It's not always advisable to pursue difficult objectives to the bitter end: there comes a point when it begins to be counter-productive.

■ There is such a thing as taking **too many** risks.

■ Independence of mind (as opposed to sheer bloody-mindedness) is often an asset, since it can help you be more flexible and original in your thinking.

Decision-making ability is not something we're born with, like the colour of our hair. It depends on skills that anyone can learn and, as our knowledge and experience grow, we can apply our skills with more efficiency and confidence year by year.

2.2 Decisions that work

No matter how carefully you think you have prepared for a decision, it doesn't always follow that it will work in practice.

It's always possible that you have **overlooked or underestimated the importance** of some vital point.

A common mistake is to misjudge the reaction of the people affected by the decision, as this case study shows.

■ Carrie had agonized over the decision of whom to appoint to the position of the hotel's night manager. She eventually chose Mario. She knew Mario was keen and ambitious, and it should be possible to overcome the man's lack of experience, provided he was given help and support. Mario had been disappointed to be turned down for promotion a few months earlier. Carrie provisionally made up her mind on Friday, thought about it all weekend and came to a final decision on Monday morning. She was ready for complaints from two of Mario's more experienced colleagues, whom she had also considered for the job.

Carrie had also worked out detailed plans, so that there would be minimum disruption when Mario switched from one job to another. So far as she could tell, she'd thought about all aspects of the decision. All that was left to be done was to tell Mario the good news.

Imagine her surprise when Mario turned down the job flat. 'Thanks for the offer, Mrs McBride, but it's impossible,' Mario said, 'I just couldn't contemplate working permanent nights.'

Activity 28

3 mins

You might say that Carrie hadn't taken into account all the factors to enable her to make a good decision. How could she have handled the issue better?

_____

_____

_____

'A man should never be ashamed to own he has been in the wrong, which is but saying, in other words, that he is wiser today than he was yesterday.'

Alexander Pope, 1727.

Perhaps you agree that, where people are going to be affected by a decision, it's highly desirable to consult them in advance. In this case, Carrie clearly went about it the wrong way. She should have handled the issue more formally and given all three potential candidates an interview. Then she would have had the opportunity to check who was genuinely in the running and who wasn't. That way she would also have avoided any risk of unfairness.

Assumptions aren't good enough: even if someone is ambitious, they won't necessarily take any job going.

It's easy to misjudge a situation, and we all make unwise decisions from time to time. When it happens, we have to think again. What is important is to learn from the experience.

3 Analysing risks and difficulties

It may seem a bit late in the day to think about risks when the decision has already been made. In *Solving Problems*, another workbook in this series, you are advised to think about risks before finally choosing the best solution to a problem.

However, in the present context the 'risks' are the dangers or damaging side effects of implementing a particular decision. These may be unavoidable, but the point is to manage and control them.

For example, if you decide to discipline a team member who has persistently been late arriving for work, you need to think about a number of things before you set about implementing your decision:

- You might handle the disciplinary issue badly, resulting in a general bad feeling.
- The team member might resent the disciplinary action, feeling it to be unfair.
- The disciplinary action might not result in any improvement in the person's performance.
- Higher levels of management might disapprove of the decision.
- Respect for your authority and judgement might be reduced.

When you are making an important decision, it makes sense to draw up a **checklist of risks**, in order to be able to counter them effectively. You might also decide to 'weight' the risks in terms of the probability of them occurring and their seriousness should they do so. This could produce a weighted table such as that below.

The 'Total' column in this table is derived by multiplying the probability of the risk occurring by the seriousness of the risk.

Risk	Probability	Seriousness	Total
Handling badly	1	8	8
Resentment	4	5	20
No improvement	3	1	3
Higher manager disapproves	2	7	14
Loss of respect	1	6	6

Activity 29

2 mins

In the table of risks above, which **two** risks should the decision maker pay most attention to?

_____

What action does this suggest the decision maker should take?

_____

_____

On the basis of the table, the two risks that need most careful attention are of the person being disciplined feeling resentful (20) and a higher manager disapproving of the decision (14).

A decision that results in further problems for the decision maker is less than perfect. It therefore makes sense to try to minimize the major risks. In this case it would be highly advisable to put some effort into:

■ thinking about how the team member's resentment could be prevented or minimized;
■ keeping higher management informed of the situation, and getting them 'on-side' before implementing the action.

Risks are often highest when a decision involves change. To find out more about this important subject, see the workbook *Leading Change.*

4 Confirming and communicating the decision

If you are about to take a decision which may have wide-ranging consequences, or which seems close to the borderline of your authority, you should **definitely** consult your manager before implementing it.

Do you know what exactly the extent of your authority is to make decisions? Perhaps it would be wise to check your job description, 'roles and responsibilities' documents etc., and to consult your manager.

You should also think about communicating your decision:

- Who will you tell, when and how?
- How much will you tell them?
- Will you give them all the same amount of detail and explanation?
- Will you tell them all in the same way?

Informing people is an important aspect of implementing a decision. If you handle this aspect badly, you might well spoil a good decision. A bad decision can actually be made worse by bad implementation.

Activity 30

6 mins

- Enzo is the manager of a sports centre. He has finally selected someone to fill the vacant role of health and safety adviser. The person has come from outside the centre. One of Enzo's own staff applied, but was not successful.

Who would Enzo inform about his decision, and how would he do so?

Who?	How?

You don't know exactly what the set-up is in Enzo's workplace, but his list would probably look something like this:

Who?	How?
The successful candidate	By phone, followed by a formal letter
The unsuccessful internal candidate	In person, followed by a formal letter
Other staff at the centre	In person at a team meeting, followed by a notice pinned on the staff noticeboard
His line manager	By memo, giving the new person's full details and an explanation of why he or she was chosen
Personnel, payroll, security departments	By memo
Customers	By putting up large notices at strategic points in the centre, in circulars going out to customers and through arranging an article in the local paper
Any specialists with whom the new person will have to deal	By letter/phone – though it might be left to the new recruit to do this part of the task

5 An action plan

The processes of analysing an issue, choosing a solution and analysing risks and resistance will suggest the actions you need to take in order to implement the decision.

In simple decisions, you can just jot these down on a piece of paper. But if the decision is important and may have many complex side-effects, you need a systematic action plan. This is because a number of different actions, involving different people and different timescales, will have to be carried out in the right order. It is no good leaving this kind of thing to guesswork.

The main aims here are to define the what, who, how and when of the various things that need to be done. In doing this you will also set your priorities for action.

Activity 31

15
mins

This Activity may provide the basis of appropriate evidence for your S/NVQ portfolio. If you are intending to take this course of action, it might be better to write your answers on separate sheets of paper.

Use the four-stage action plan below to plot the implementation of an important decision that you will be taking in the near future (this could be a leisure- or home-based issue, as well as a work-based one).

Stage 1.   What actions?

List **all** the principal actions required. Don't forget the communication aspects, which are essential to gaining the co-operation of team and colleagues and minimizing unwanted side-effects.

Stage 2.   When and in what order?

Re-arrange the actions in their logical order.

For example, 'brief team on new arrangements for monitoring quality' must come before 'retrain team in new quality procedures', but after 'agree new arrangements for monitoring quality with production manager'.

Stage 3.   How long?

Next, think about how long each action is going to take (including preparation time – a team briefing may only take a few minutes, but preparation for it can take days).

Often the time you feel you need will be longer than you feel you can afford. Save time by planning two or more actions to run in parallel, where possible.

Stage 4.   Who and how?

Indicate who is to do what and when, and also, where appropriate:

- the methods to be used;
- the resources required;
- any special considerations;
- whether other actions are affected.

You can adapt this plan to your particular needs and use it to help you with the implementation of your decisions.

Action plan for:
Action
Start date
Finish date
By whom
Method
Resources required
Special needs
Also affects

6 Evaluating the outcome

In Session A a good decision was defined as:

the optimum decision (i.e. the best all-round in terms of simplicity, side-effects, gain etc.) that at least meets the minimum objectives.

How can you tell whether your decisions, which you have carefully prepared, made and implemented, are working in these terms?

Activity 32

5 mins

One obvious option is to draw up a checklist of questions about how well the decision has worked.

What questions would you consider relevant?

_____

_____

_____

_____

_____

_____

The response to this activity can be found on page 80.

Depending on the nature of the issue and the decision, you might also want to consider:

■ how long the decision remained effective (the effect of policy and organizational changes sometimes wears off after a period, either because people lose interest or because other changes make it irrelevant);
■ whether the time and energy put into the decision was justified by the benefits it produced;
■ whether it has produced any benefits that you hadn't anticipated.

Perhaps the acid test for any decision is:

Would I make the same decision again?

Self-assessment 4

1   Three factors seem to be involved in a person's ability to 'get things done'.
    What are they?

    _____

    _____

    _____

2   Put the parts of this jumbled passage back in the right order.

    a   and we all make unwise decisions
    b   from time to time.
    c   have to think again.
    d   It's easy to
    e   learn from the experience.
    f   misjudge a situation,
    g   What is important is to
    h   When it happens, we

    Correct order: _____

3   When you compile a 'risk weighting table', what **two** factors should you rate
    against each risk?

    _____

    _____

4   In the passage below every fourth word has been removed. Replace the
    missing words so that the text makes sense.

    Choose from these words:

    and,   but,   from,
    is,   main,   only,
    to,   whether,   you,

    A brilliant solution _____ a tricky problem _____

    no good unless _____ can implement it, _____ one of the

    _____ difficulties is resistance _____ other people.

Answers to these questions can be found on page 79.

7 Summary

- Decision-making ability is not something we're born with, like the colour of our hair; it depends on skills that anyone can learn and, as your knowledge and experience grow, you can apply your skills with more efficiency and confidence year by year.

- Even the best-prepared decisions don't always work. It's always possible that you have **overlooked or underestimated the importance** of some vital point.

- A common mistake is to misjudge the reaction of the people affected by the decision.

- When you are making an important decision, it makes sense to draw up a **checklist of risks**, in order to be able to counter them effectively. You might also decide to 'weight' the risks in terms of the probability of them occurring and their seriousness should they do so.

- Typical resistance points to a decision include:

  - resentment or non-compliance by the individuals concerned;
  - objections from higher management;
  - lack of cash resources to carry it through;
  - lack of enthusiasm for a solution by those who actually have to implement it;
  - lack of the skills and training needed to implement it.

- It is often useful to draw up an action plan for implementing more complex decisions. This will show who is to do what and when, and also, where appropriate:

  - the methods to be used;
  - the resources required;
  - any special considerations;
  - whether other actions are affected.

- When evaluating your decision, the main point is to check the outcomes against the specific objectives. The acid test is perhaps to ask **'would I make the same decision again?'**

Performance checks

1 Quick quiz

Jot down answers to the following questions on *Making and Taking Decisions.*

Question 1   You lack the relevant experience; time is short; the situation is non-routine. What sort of a decision do these factors point to?

a _____ decision.

Question 2   What is the definition of a good decision?

_____

Question 3   When can it be wise to postpone a decision?

_____

Question 4   What is an 'optimization' or 'improvement' problem?

_____

Question 5   There are three advantages of putting an issue or problem down in writing. Name **one** of them.

_____

Question 6   What's wrong with this statement:

'Your desired outcomes are what your decision will deliver.'

_____

Question 7   What are 'GO/NO-GO criteria'?

_____

Question 8   What are 'constraints' on a decision?

_____

65

Question 9   Complete this sentence, which explains some of the difficulties that decision-makers often face.

Most decisions have to be made with i_____ i_____.

Question 10   The information on which you base a decision needs to be relevant, reliable, accurate – and what else?

_____

Question 11   Decisions often need to be tested for feasibility. What would a study of economic feasibility tell you?

_____

Question 12   What factors would a study of social feasibility consider?

_____

Question 13   There's a simple and practical way to bring out the pros and cons of a decision option. What is it?

_____

Question 14   Choose the most appropriate statement from these four remarks about the risk side of decision making:

a   Decisions involve risks – the more the better.   ☐

b   Decision makers must balance risks and benefits.   ☐

c   The bigger the decision, the more risks must be taken.   ☐

d   Managers cannot be seen to take risks.   ☐

Question 15   What is the acid test for the success of any decision you have made?

_____

Answers to these questions can be found on page 81.

2 Workbook assessment

60 mins

Read the following case study and then deal with the questions that follow. Write your answers on a separate sheet of paper.

■ Lettie Manning is supervisor to a workteam of fifteen people in a supermarket distribution warehouse.

A two-shift system is in operation: the first shift runs from 7 am to 2 pm, the second from 1 pm to 8 pm.

The team's main task is to pack food items for distribution to a chain of supermarkets. Conveyor belts are used to move the goods from the storage area to the outgoing collection areas. The team's normal throughput rate is around 10,000 items an hour. With breaks for meals etc., the line runs for twelve hours a day.

Lettie's manager arrives one Friday afternoon and tells her that, when two new supermarket branches are opened in a month's time, it is estimated that the warehouse will need to ship 150,000 items a day.

Lettie is asked to make plans to deal with this increase in throughput rate. Any options will be considered, but as usual, cost will be a **major** consideration.

■ What problems might Lettie foresee as a result of this change?

■ What decisions will Lettie have to make in putting forward her proposals?

■ What are the constraints on these decisions?

■ How can Lettie best define the desired outcome of these decisions?

■ What further information might you require if you were making these decisions yourself?

■ From the description above, what would you say were Lettie's best options?

Portfolio of evidence CI.I, DI.I

3 Work-based assignment

60 mins

The time guide for this assignment gives you an approximate idea of how long it is likely to take you to write up your findings. You will find you need to spend some additional time gathering information, talking to colleagues and thinking about the assignment. The result of your efforts should be presented on separate sheets of paper.

Your written response to this assignment may form useful evidence for your S/NVQ portfolio. The assignment is designed to help you demonstrate the following Personal Comptences:

■ thinking and taking decisions;
■ influencing others.

From the list you made for Activity 4, choose **three** important decisions you have had to make recently during the course of your work.

For each decision, note down:

a how you went about making the decision (be specific about whom you consulted, what information you gathered, and how, what techniques you used, etc.);

b how successful the decisions turned out to be (explain how you evaluated the decisions and make sure to note any unexpected outcomes, both negative and positive);

c choose just **one** of these three decisions and explain in detail how, with the benefit of both hindsight and what you have learned in this workbook, you would now go about tackling the decision. Base your notes on our decision-making formula:

I   state the **issue** or problem
O   decide **objectives**
C   identify **constraints**
I   collect **information**
O   evaluate **options**
I   **implement** the best option
O   evaluate the **outcome**.

Reflect and review

Now that you have completed your work on *Making and Taking Decisions*, let us review the workbook objectives.

Our first objective was:

■ You will be better able to adopt a systematic and thoughtful approach to making difficult decisions.

The whole workbook was aimed at encouraging you to take a systematic approach by following the seven-stage decision-making formula:

I   state the **issue** or problem
O decide **objectives**
C identify **constraints**
I   collect **information**
O evaluate **options**
I   **implement** the best option
O evaluate the **outcome**.

As a manager, team leader or supervisor, you have a responsibility to make the best decisions that you can, and this formula provides a framework. Nevertheless, everyone's style and situation are different, and you may well find that there are some stages that you tend to skimp or even ignore.

You may want to ask yourself:

■ Which stages do I feel least happy with, or tend to try to minimize?

_____

_____

■ If I make a habit of this, what disadvantages might there be?

_____

_____

_____

69

The second workbook objective was as follows:

■ You will be better able to understand what makes good and bad decisions.

In this workbook you have looked at how a 'good' decision might be defined and at some of the factors that make decisions good or bad. Bad decisions are those that fail to achieve the desired outcomes and specific objectives that you set. Then there are those that not only do not succeed but actually make things worse.

The factors that lead to bad decisions include:

■ being unsystematic in your approach;
■ not getting enough information;
■ being in too much of a hurry;
■ failing to consider the constraints;
■ failing to consider the risks;
■ failing to consult and communicate with people whose consent and help you need.

■ Thinking about those 'bad decision' factors, do you think you have any bad decision-making habits that you ought to try to remedy?

_____

_____

That brings us to the next two objectives:

■ You will be better able to set and prioritize objectives for decisions.

■ You will be better able to identify constraints on your decisions.

Both of these are key aspects of reaching a good decision. If you don't consider the constraints, you will end up with decisions that can't be implemented, or which are high-risk and expensive (in both time and money) to action. If you don't set your objectives properly, you won't have a clear focus for your decisions, and you won't be able to evaluate them properly afterwards.

■ Objective-setting is particularly important and useful in a wide range of management activities. It is well worth becoming expert at doing it. Think about the other kinds of situations where it would help to have clear and measurable objectives and list a few of them here.

_____

_____

_____

_____

70

The next objective was:

■ You will be better able to develop and evaluate decision options.

This workbook doesn't say a great deal about developing the options (there is more about this in another workbook in the series, *Solving Problems*). Suffice to say that when you have consulted, gathered information and considered the constraints, there will usually be at least two options for every issue or problem. The important point is to evaluate them thoroughly. You looked at various ways of doing this: through numerical methods, using computer spreadsheets and by considering the risks attached to each option.

■ When you are reaching a decision, is anything holding you back from making a thorough evaluation of the options? If so, what?

_____

_____

_____

Perhaps you feel that you don't have the skill, the information or the time. But whatever is holding you back, you must work to overcome it. No two decisions are exactly identical in their outcomes, and if one option is only 5 per cent better than another, you need to know. It is out of these 'five per cents' here and there that commercial and career success are built.

The final objective was this:

■ You will be better able to implement decisions and evaluate outcomes.

Skill in decision making is something that you can learn and which improves with experience. Here is a checklist that you can use whenever you've made and implemented a decision:

> ■ Did I correctly identify the original issue or problem?
> ■ Was it a problem that I could have identified and dealt with earlier?
> ■ Did I set appropriate objectives?
> ■ Were the options that I developed reasonable ones in the circumstances?
> ■ Did I correctly identify the constraints on my decision?
> ■ Did I accurately evaluate the options?
> ■ Was my decision the best one in the circumstances?
> ■ Did I implement it effectively?
> ■ Have I evaluated it properly?

As you ask and answer each question, make a note of:

- anything that didn't go quite right;
- anything you failed to do or failed to spot;
- anything you spent time on that wasn't worth it;
- anything you would do better next time.

What have you learned? Should you tackle the next decision differently? What extra skills, knowledge and resources do you need in order to do better next time?

Remember that:

- the better you know your job,
- the better you know your team,
- the better you know how your organization works,
- the more decisions you make,

the easier and better your decisions will become.

2 Action plan

Use this plan to further develop for yourself a course of action you want to take. Make a note in the left-hand column of the issues or problems you want to tackle, and then decide what you intend to do, and make a note in Column 2.

The resources you need might include time, materials, information or money. You may need to negotiate for some of them, but they could be something easily acquired, like half an hour of somebody's time, or a chapter of a book. Put whatever you need in Column 3. No plan means anything without a timescale, so put a realistic target completion date in Column 4.

Finally, describe the outcome you want to achieve as a result of this plan, whether it is for your own benefit or advancement, or a more efficient way of doing things.

Desired outcomes

1 Issues	2 Action	3 Resources	4 Target completion

Actual outcomes

3 Extensions

Extension 1

Book   *The New Rational Manager*
Authors   Charles H. Kepner and Benjamin B. Tregoe
Edition   2nd edition 1981
Publisher   Kepner-Tregoe Inc.

You may be interested in finding out more about problem solving and decision making using weighting and other numerical techniques. If so, you might consider taking up this extension, a simple but fascinating book subtitled 'A systematic approach to problem solving and decision making'. It is the fruit of many years' practical experience by US management consultants Kepner-Tregoe Inc., and it contains a number of case studies which have become rather famous. These case histories are useful in themselves, but the real lesson of the Kepner-Tregoe approach is that even the most mysterious problems can be solved by careful analysis of information.

Extension 2

Information sources typically available to people in management roles.

■ The workteam

An excellent source of information, especially when it comes to specific work issues. After all, the team members are often the people who have to deal with the problems first hand.

■ Your line manager

Your immediate superior is of course a good source of information, particularly on tasks that he or she has assigned you. A good line manager will usually be happy to supply all the information available.

■ Other managers and supervisors

Colleagues often face the same kinds of problems that you do and have experience and knowledge that can help. 'Networking' with other managers and supervisors and regularly exchanging information with them will pay dividends.

■ Internal documents

These include all sorts of rule books, operational manuals, procedural guidelines, policy documents (e.g. the health and safety policy document), technical drawings, lists of approved suppliers, catalogues, brochures and price lists, and not least **reports** on incidents, disputes and other issues that have arisen in the past.

■ Internal management information

Many organizations now generate a large amount of information via their computer systems. This includes performance data (sales, costs, output, productivity, wastage etc.) and especially financial data (performance against budgets). Information about the future (such as business plans and forecasts) may also be available.

■ Specialists in the organization

Many organizations have specialist departments and people who provide information and advice to their colleagues. These may include the personnel department (for all matters affecting employment), the safety officer, the legal department (in larger companies), the computer or information technology department, the drawing office, the publications department and others, depending on the nature of the organization.

■ Customers and suppliers

Invaluable sources of information, customers can tell you what they want and what is going right (or, more likely, wrong). Suppliers possess vast amounts of data and expertise about their products and their applications.

■ Libraries and information services

Larger organizations have libraries; if yours doesn't, try your public library. For technical matters, a trade or industry association may provide an information service.

■ Official publications

There are numerous official publications, including British Standards and the many thousands of books and papers published by HM Stationery Office. Your local library should be able to help you with these.

■ External computer databases

There are now lots of these, available through the Internet or as specialized subscription services. If your organization does not subscribe to the relevant ones, your local library or trade/industry organization might.

Extension 3

Book	*Mastering Spreadsheets, Budgets and Forecasting*
Author	Malcolm Secrett
Edition	1st edition 1993
Publisher	Pitman

Computer spreadsheet programs are ideal for working out the detailed cost and revenue implications of decisions. A well-constructed spreadsheet can enable you to ask all kinds of 'what if?' questions: What if we price the new product at £24.99 instead of £22.99? What if the costs are 15 per cent higher than we expect? and so on. There are plenty of sources for learning the basics of using spreadsheets (check with your library). If you would like to develop your spreadsheet skills further, you may like to take up this extension, which focuses on budgets and forecasts.

These Extensions can be taken up via your NEBS Management Centre. They will either have them or will arrange that you have access to them. However, it may be more convenient to check out the materials with your personnel or training people at work – they may well give you access. There are other good reasons for approaching your own people; for example, they will become aware of your interest and you can involve them in your development.

4 Answers to self-assessment questions

Self-assessment 1 on page 16

1 a Decisions mostly involve making **judgements**, based on **understanding**. The better your understanding, the better chance you have of making sound **judgements**.

  b Decisions are harder when:

   ■ you lack the relevant **experience**;
   ■ you can't see clear **choices**;
   ■ other **people** are involved;
   ■ there are many **aspects** to consider;
   ■ **time** is short;
   ■ a lot is riding on the **decision**;
   ■ the situation is non-**routine**.

  c No one decision-making **style** is appropriate for all circumstances.

2 a As a general rule, you shouldn't waste time on decision making until a problem has reached a point where you can no longer ignore it.

   This is FALSE. Effective managers watch out for potential problems and deal with them early, before they become troublesome.

  b Apparently effortless decisions made about complex subjects are invariably based on being clever.

   This is FALSE. When someone makes difficult decisions with ease, it's usually because they are used to making decisions of that kind.

  c Doing nothing is never an option.

   This is FALSE. Sometimes doing nothing is the best option.

  d A manager who is too 'democratic' may sometimes find that required decisions take much longer than desired.

   This is TRUE.

3 The two of the four statements which reflect the most common reason for making wrong decisions are:

a acting without thought;
b not having enough information.

The other two statements may account for some wrong decisions, but having too many options or too much time is not necessarily a disadvantage.

Self-assessment 2 on page 33

1 a Beware of becoming so concerned about **small** problems that you lose sight of the **big** ones.

b MUSTs are your **minimum** objectives, which we can also think of as GO/NO-GO **criteria**.

c Giving non-**essential** objectives a numerical **weighting** will often help you to reach your decision.

d Making decisions usually means making **compromises**. Few decisions leave all parties feeling completely satisfied with the **outcome**.

2 a You can anticipate problems by being observant.

This is perfectly true. Good managers, supervisors and team leaders are always monitoring, observing, comparing, listening and thinking ahead, ready to spot and act on small changes in the human and physical environment

b Writing a problem down is not as helpful as talking it over with someone.

This is not the case, because both are equally useful. It is less important **how** the problem is expressed, as long as it **is** expressed.

c You may often be constrained by lack of resources, but should not be constrained by the demands of the workteam.

No, the demands of the workteam can sometimes be the most important aspect of an issue.

d When your manager says 'You have a completely free hand', it means there will be absolutely no constraints on the decision you make.

This may appear to be true, but it is very rare for there to be no constraints on a decision, whatever your manager or anyone else says about it.

3 a state the **issue** or problem
b decide **objectives**
c identify **constraints**
d collect **information**
e evaluate **option**s
f **implement** the best option
g evaluate the **outcome**

77

4 The two major benefits of setting specific objectives are as follows:

a You know what you are trying to achieve, so you can focus on this and there's less chance of being side-tracked.

b When you've made and implemented your decision, you can measure how well you've done.

Self-assessment 3 on page 48

1 The statements go together like this:

a Before you go on to evaluate your options it's worth checking whether **[z] colleagues, team members or your line manager have any suggestions to add.**

b Decisions involving money and output cannot be **[v] made without making lots of numerical calculations.**

c Managers often feel that they have **[x] much more information than they can cope with.**

d Most decisions have to be **[w] made with imperfect information.**

e The workteam is often one of the best **[y] sources of information for the supervisor.**

2 The completed diagram should look like this:

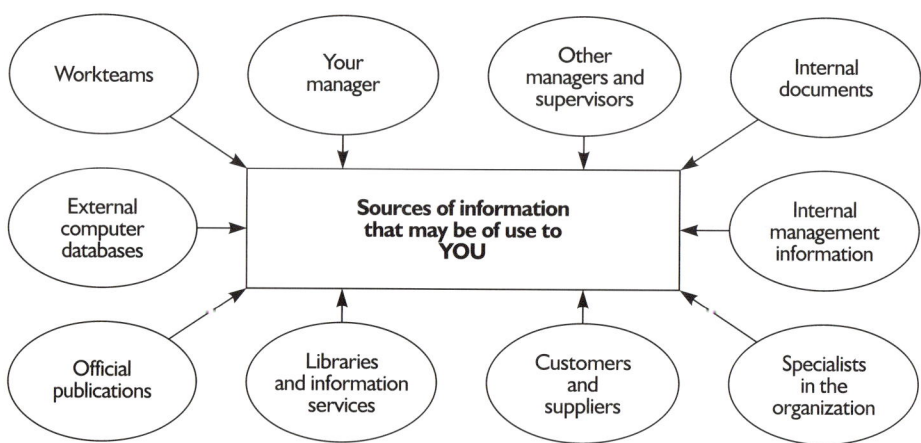

3 The four aspects of feasibility studies are:

- social;
- technical;
- economic;
- environmental.

4 The passage should read:

In order to assess the **quality** of information, you need to ask:

- Is the information **relevant**?
- Is it **reliable**?
- Is it **accurate**?
- Is it sufficiently **comprehensive** (in quantity and detail)?

5   If you have gone through all the steps of the decision-making formula systematically and you still can't decide which solution to a problem would be the best option, then **get a friend or colleague to champion one option, while you argue for another. This may bring out weaknesses and strengths not appreciated before**

Self-assessment 4 on page 62

1   The three factors that seem to be involved in a person's ability to 'get things done' are:

- the individual's personality, experience and skills;
- the culture within which they operate; and
- the demands of the particular situation they face.

2   The correct order is **d**, **f**, **a**, **b**, **h**, **c**, **g**, **e**. The passage should read like this:

It's easy to misjudge a situation, and we all make unwise decisions from time to time. When it happens, we have to think again. What is important is to learn from the experience.

3   The factors you should rate in a risk weighting table are:

- the probability of the risks occurring
- their seriousness if they do.

4   A brilliant solution **to** a tricky problem **is** no good unless **you** can implement it, **and** one of the **main** difficulties is resistance **from** other people.

5 Answers to activities

Activity 19 on page 32

1   There is a conflict between the drive to increase production and (a) the need to maintain quality and (b) constraints on working speeds set by safety considerations.

2   There is a potential conflict between the desire to increase production and the fact that the supervisor doesn't control the supply of parts.

3   To achieve higher production the supervisor needs to spend more time motivating her team and dealing with their problems. This is constrained by the need to spend time liaising with other teams and reporting to her manager.

Activity 24 on page 45

Here are some more suggestions for solving Mina's problem:

- Subcontracting some or all of the packing to another firm.
- Using homeworkers. This would involve extra administration in shipping soap and materials to various local addresses and collecting finished packs for despatch. It would, however, suit people who can't work full-time or can't travel to work, and the low pay might not be such an issue.
- Mechanizing some or all of the processes.

In fact the last two ideas were initially ruled out as being unworkable. Eventually, however, all the others were also eliminated and the firm signed up some homeworkers. This has worked very well, and the firm has also made provisional plans for using machines to pack the soap.

Activity 25 on page 46

The questions might include these:

- What will be the effects on staffing numbers?
- What training will be needed?
- What new work-patterns will be needed?
- Will there be resistance to the proposed changes, and, if so, how can it be overcome?

Activity 26 on page 47

Here are some further questions that you could ask:

- Do I know enough about the effects of these options?
- Which option is most likely to provide my desired outcome?
- Has the problem changed as a result of my investigations and increased knowledge?
- Would it help to express the problem differently?
- Do I need more information?
- Do I need more ideas?
- Do I need help from others affected by the decision?
- Have I really kept an open mind, or did I have one option in mind all along, which has now turned out to be less attractive?
- Could more than one option be chosen, or a combination of two or more?

Activity 32 on page 61

Checklist for evaluating how well your decision has worked:

- Were the MUST objectives (the minimum objectives) met?
- To what extent were the WANT/WOULD LIKE objectives met? (You would want to refer back to your full list of objectives here.)
- Did I succeed in informing the right people at the right time?
- Did I correctly identify the risks and difficulties associated with the decision?
- Did the action I took to minimize the risks and difficulties work?
- Did implementing this decision give rise to any new problems that I hadn't anticipated?

6 Answers to the quick quiz

Answer 1   These factors point to a **difficult** decision.

Answer 2   In Session A a good decision was defined as **the optimum decision that at least meets the minimum objectives**.

Answer 3   It can sometimes be wise to postpone a decision **when you don't have sufficient information on which to base it**.

Answer 4   An 'optimization' or 'improvement' problem is **where an opportunity exists to get the most from a situation**.

Answer 5   The three advantages of putting an issue or problem down in writing are:

- it forces you to think;
- it gives you a clear statement on which you can focus your attention;
- it helps you see where the main difficulties lie.

Answer 6   The problem with this statement is that there is often a big difference between your **desired outcomes** and the **actual** outcomes. It would make more sense to say 'Your desired outcomes are what you **expect** your decision to deliver'.

Answer 7   'GO/NO-GO criteria' are those objectives that a decision **must** deliver if it is to be successful.

Answer 8   Constraints are the **factors that limit and restrict our options** when considering what decision to make.

Answer 9   Most decisions have to be made with **imperfect information**.

Answer 10   The information on which you base a decision needs to be relevant, reliable, accurate and **sufficiently comprehensive** (in quantity and detail).

Answer 11   A study of economic feasibility would tell you how **beneficial the decision would be in financial terms** (i.e. how much it would earn or save, compared with how much it would cost).

Answer 12   A study of social feasibility would consider **the impact of the decision on the people involved**.

Answer 13   A simple and practical way to bring out the pros and cons of a decision option is to **argue it out with a friend or colleague**.

Answer 14   Having worked through this workbook, you should have selected statement b as the most appropriate: **Decision makers must balance risks and benefits**.

Answer 15   The acid test is **'Would I make the same decision again?'**

7 Certificate

Completion of this certificate by an authorized person shows that you have worked through all the parts of this workbook and satisfactorily completed the assessments. The certificate provides a record of what you have done that may be used for exemptions or as evidence of prior learning against other nationally certificated qualifications.

Pergamon Open Learning and NEBS Management are always keen to refine and improve their products. One of the key sources of information to help this process are people who have just used the product. If you have any information or views, good or bad, please pass these on.

NEBS
MANAGEMENT
DEVELOPMENT

SUPER **SERIES**

THIRD EDITION

Making and Taking Decisions

....

has satisfactorily completed this workbook

Name of signatory ....

Position ....

Signature ....

Date ....

Official stamp

SUPER SERIES

SUPER SERIES 3

To Order - phone us direct for prices and availability details
(please quote ISBNs when ordering)
College orders: 01865 314333 • Account holders: 01865 314301
Individual purchases: 01865 314627 (please have credit card details ready)

We Need Your Views

We really need your views in order to make the Super Series 3 (SS3) an even better learning tool for you. Please take time out to complete and return this questionnaire to Tessa Gingell, Pergamon Open Learning, Linacre House, Jordan Hill, Oxford, OX2 8BR.

Name : ....

Address : ....

....

Company & Position (if applicable) : ....

Title of workbook : ....

If applicable, please state which qualification you are studying for. If not, please describe what study you are undertaking, and with which organisation or college:

....

Please grade the following out of 10 (10 being extremely good, 0 being extremely poor):

Content	....	Appropriateness to your position	....
Readability	....	Qualification coverage	....

What did you particularly like about this workbook?

Are there any features you disliked about this workbook? Please identify them.

Are there any errors we have missed? If so, please state page number: ....

How are you using the material? For example, as an open learning course, as a reference resource, as a training resource etc.

....

How did you hear about Super Series 3?:

Word of mouth: Through my tutor/trainer: Mailshot:

Other (please give details): ....

Many thanks for your help in returning this form.